Kingdom Issues:

More Hopeful Compositions
from Partway Up the Mountain

Steve Elderbrock

Parson's Porch Books

www.parsonsporchbooks.com

Kingdom Issues: More Hopeful Compositions from Partway Up the Mountain

ISBN: Softcover 978-1-951472-38-2

To

Deb, Kate, and **Gussie** –

three of my biggest supporters.

Contents

I. What's Past is Prologue

II. More Recent Ramblings

III. Reflections on the Lord's Prayer

I. What's Past is Prologue

Location, Location, Location

Psalm 84; John 6:56-69

August 23, 2009

My sermon title comes from that well-known, maybe apocryphal, mantra of every real estate agent: "Location, location, location."

I don't know if there really is anything to that mantra when it comes to real estate, but there is something to that in terms of our faith. I'm not just speaking of physical location here, but as a spiritual idea, in terms of where we find ourselves on the journey of faith. I find this idea emerging in both of today's Scripture readings: location is important.

This is particularly evident in Psalm 84. This Psalm is thought to have been written by pilgrims on their way up to Jerusalem, to the Temple, God's house. How lovely is your dwelling place, O God. Happy are those who live in your house, who worship and sing praise to you there. Better is a day in your court than a thousand days anywhere else. I'd rather be a doorkeeper in the house of the Lord than live in the most elaborate tent imaginable or in a castle of wickedness.

The Hebrew people at the time this Psalm was composed were talking about a physical location. This is a Psalm about the Temple in Jerusalem. We read last week the story of Solomon building the Temple. Before that the Hebrew people located God's presence in the ark of the covenant, which we all know from Indiana Jones, in which were placed the tablets of the Ten Commandments and samples of manna and some other artifacts indicative of God's presence with God's people. It was thought that God's presence, which during the exodus went ahead of the people in a cloud by day and a pillar of fire by night, came to rest in the ark of the covenant. And then when the Temple was finally built, the ark was placed in the Holy of Holies and God came literally sat down upon the ark—it served as a throne for God, where God sat in God's Temple, the place where God lived. Thus we have a very real, very literal idea of God's physical presence and God's location. This is where I AM is. "Let us go to the House of God." So people would make an annual pilgrimage to this specific location where God lived—to pay their respects and offer their burnt offerings. Location, location, location.

What's left in Jerusalem today are some remains of the wall of the Temple Mount upon which the Temple once stood. Actually twice stood and was twice destroyed if you remember your history. The First Temple built by Solomon was destroyed by the Babylonians in 586 B.C., and then under Zerubbabel and others after the Babylonian exile between 520 and 515 B.C., the Second Temple was built to replace the First one. It was this Second Temple that King Herod, almost 500 years later, enlarged and expanded, and it was Herod's Temple which Jesus himself visited and where he worshiped. Herod's temple was destroyed by the Romans in 70 A.D. There are still in Jerusalem, and I have seen them for myself, some huge rocks and debris left from that destruction of 70 A.D., still laying where they fell. This spot remains holy to the Jews, though, this place where God's Temple once stood and where God once lived.

That physical location is still holy to the Jewish people, as well as to Muslims and Christians. But Jesus, in John's Gospel, takes this idea to a deeper level. Jesus says: "I am the bread of life. If you eat my body and drink my blood you abide in me and I abide in you." Notice the shift – Jesus isn't talking about a physical location; he's talking about himself. "Abide in my and I will abide in you, I will live and well in you, with you." This is where things start to get difficult, at least for his disciples. It is the idea that God does not dwell in one particular place, but that now God dwells in a particular person, Jesus Christ, and even more difficult perhaps for the disciples to get their minds around, God can through Jesus come to dwell in us, too. We don't have to travel to a certain location and make an annual pilgrimage to see God, God is with us wherever we go, in whatever location we find ourselves.

Jesus tells his disciples in another passage that the Holy Spirit will come and guide them, and us. The Holy Spirit in some sense replaces the necessity of a Temple. The Spirit comes to us, so we don't have to travel up to Jerusalem to find God (of course there is still very good reason to go to Jerusalem, and if you ever get that opportunity, take it.) God is present with you, so you don't have to find God in any particular location, except right where you are. God has already found you. In some ways this is not an easy message to hear, especially for these first-century followers of Jesus, most of whom were Jewish, as he was. With the Temple still intact, standing, and the center of Jewish religious life, this message that God was with and in Jesus, and could dwell in us, well, that was a bit surprising, if not scandalous.

I always chuckle when I hear the crowd's response to Jesus saying these things in John 6, because it is a response some people still have to sermons today: "That's difficult, that's hard to hear, I'm not sure I can accept that." I've said before that Jesus was not a good salesman. If Jesus were the pastor of your church, many people would be upset, honestly. "He keeps driving people away!" That's what was happening there in John chapter 6 – people were beginning to drift away from Jesus and his difficult, almost scandalous message. So Jesus turns to his disciples, the twelve, his closest followers, and asks them this profound question: "Do you also wish to go away?" And Simon Peter, in one of those wonderful moments when he just blurts out an answer straight from his heart, poses an even profounder question, as well as a beautiful statement of faith, in response: "Lord, to whom can we go? Where are we going to go? You, and only you, have the words of eternal life."

Again notice the shift here in these readings, from "God how lovely is your dwelling place" to "Where and to whom can we go?" Where are we going to go, except to Jesus, the one who has the words and who is The Word of eternal life. This is a spiritual locating rather than a physical one – God not in a specific place but in a person and in us, with us. We don't need to travel to any specific place to see God or encounter God. We do need to set our hearts and our lives and our path on the same path as God, the path walked by and preached about by Jesus. To follow a person not to go to a place. It's a pilgrimage that is not just annual or weekly, but lifelong and constant, as we set our course on a person and his teachings and his example, not set a course for any special location. It is a matter of accepting the gift that Jesus brought and following in his footsteps. Walking with him wherever he leads us, to whatever location or place, even if that location ends up being right where we already are. A spiritual pilgrimage not a physical one. An everyday walk with Jesus, an everyday walk with God.

That's the paradigm shift we see in these two readings.

I mentioned on my first Sunday back from my recent Sabbatical, part of which I spent in Israel and specifically in Jerusalem, that I didn't want to discourage anyone from going to these incredible places, these holy places - and yes, we Christians have our Holy Places. And I'm sure in your own life you have your holy places, too – places that feel especially holy to you, locations where you feel especially close to God and especially aware of God's presence. Such locations are valuable, and we need them. But the point is that even if we didn't have such places, we would still have God close by. We don't need to go anywhere beyond our own hearts to find God.

Of course we need to stay with God - that is part of our task. So let me leave you by posing once again those questions posed in John's gospel today and invite you to ponder them for yourself and in your life this week: "Do you also wish to go away?" Do you wish to go away from the rather difficult path that Jesus has set for us, for each of us? "But where will you go, and to whom will you go instead?" Only Jesus has the words of eternal life. And there are two other questions which I think grow out of all this:

Where are you located right now on your journey of faith?

And are you where God wants you to be?

Amen.

This Man

Psalm 16; Acts 2:14, 22-32

2nd Sunday of Easter
May 1, 2011

This morning we are reminded that Easter is not limited to one day a year, but it is a season, and in fact our whole lives are lived in the wake of Easter. But sometimes after we've celebrated it so often the message of Easter can begin to seem a little abstract. Concepts like "new life," "resurrection," and "salvation" which are so much a part of Easter can seem kind of vague and removed from daily life. But Scripture never lets us forget the particular, specific nature of our salvation and the particular, specific person at the center of all of this, through whom we were saved.

That's part of the message of Peter's Easter sermon which was recorded in Acts 2. I also think that is the message of today's Psalm, which focuses our attention on a particular person, our Lord and Savior, this man Jesus of Nazareth, so that we will never forgot that our salvation is a very particular thing that was given to us in a particular time and place and person – a person who reaches across time to us. This man, this Jesus - as Peter says repeatedly in his sermon - this man who was born at a certain time and in a certain place, this man who lived and walked among us, who taught, who preached, who healed, who laughed, who cried, who ate, who drank – this man, who, as we say in the Apostles' Creed "was born of the Virgin Mary, suffered under Pontius Pilate, was crucified, died, and was buried" – this man, Peter says to the people in Jerusalem that day, this Jesus of Nazareth who you helped kill, this man who we all betrayed and turned upon, this man who died and who God raised from the dead – this man was the means of our salvation, this particular, specific human being: Jesus Christ.

There are lots of reasons to keep our focus on this particular person, Jesus. Remembering, of course, that Jesus was more than just a man, more than just a human being, he was also God, fully human but also fully divine. Attention to Jesus as a particular person can keep us from being distracted by what Psalm 16 calls: "other gods." If anyone else ever comes to you claiming to be your savior, claiming to have all the answers, just remember that particular person who we know was our Savior and did have the answers, Jesus Christ of Nazareth. This reminder keeps us from being distracted by those claiming to be what Jesus truly was and still is. If we ever begin sensing that we are putting our hope in anything other than this man, Jesus, we have all these reminders in Scripture to pull us back. No one else, nothing else, can save but this particular person, this man Jesus.

Of course this is part of the scandal of our faith as well. Even Jesus had trouble convincing people that he, this particular man, was the Messiah. You may remember when Jesus went to his hometown, he wasn't received very well because they already knew him, as a particular person – how could this Jesus, son of Mary and Joseph, be the Messiah? "I remember teaching him in Sunday School." "I remember him jumping over the backs of the pews or crawling underneath them." "I remember putting a Band-Aid on his knee when he fell off his bike." "I remember that time he banged his thumb with a hammer trying to help his Dad in his carpentry shop." How could this man, this Jesus, be the Messiah?

This threw a lot of people off. And I think his particularity still throws some people off. This man is the Savior, our Messiah? This particular human being? "Hmmm, he isn't quite what I imagined; I sort of pictured him differently." The people of Jesus's time expected the Messiah to look and behave differently than Jesus did. I think some of them were, honestly, a little disappointed. They wanted a messiah who would come riding into town on a white horse, swinging a sword, slaying all their enemies. Some of us today still harbor those same expectations and disappointments. This Jesus? I thought he'd be different, I expected someone taller, I expected him to have blue eyes, I expected someone from a better family, someone better dressed. I expected the Messiah to talk more about victory and triumph and less about love and wishy-washy stuff like that. This man? This Jesus?

Maybe part of the problem is that when you've waited so long for something, and you've built up your expectations so high, when it finally comes, when you finally get it, the reality of it can be a little disappointing compared to your dreams and expectations. I remember being a kid waiting for Christmas…well, waiting for the Christmas presents, to be honest. You know that one particular gift you had been waiting and hoping for, and then on Christmas day you unwrap it and…well, it looks smaller and not quite the same as it did in the ad on TV. And within 8 minutes you had broken it. Did you ever order anything from those ads in the back of comic books? The X-ray glasses or the secret decoder ring or those sea monkeys, and then you wait and wait, you check the mailbox every day, and then when it arrives it is just a cheap plastic thing or some brine shrimp eggs. Totally different than as advertised and expected.

Sometimes we might wish Jesus was different than he is – that he said different things, acted a different way, maybe that he'd settled down and gotten married and been a better American. You know Jesus never once even mentions America? Hard to believe. But here's this man, this Jesus, talking about loving enemies and turning the other cheek and taking up a cross. This Jesus, who he was, what he said, what he did – that's who our Savior is. Always and forever. That can be tough for some people to accept. They'd rather wait for another, newer version – Jesus 2.0.

Not to mention the fact that our Savior was a man, a human being, like us. That in and of itself is pretty scandalous for some. God becoming one of us? With hair and wrinkles and halitosis and "naughty bits"? Hmmm. Yet again and again and again Scripture draws us back to this fact – this unexpected and even scandalous fact – that this man, this Jesus IS our Savior. There's not another one coming. We're stuck with the Savior we have been given. Take him or leave him. Of course the real irony is that this particular man, this Jesus, despite all appearances, is much better than we could have ever expected, much better than we could ever have hoped for.

Notice all the wonderful things Psalm 16 reminds us about our Lord and notice as well how often the Psalm uses the word "you," a very specific pronoun. Not the Southern "y'all," but "you," my particular, specific Lord. "In you, I take refuge." "Apart from you I have no good thing." "You have assigned me my portion and my cup; you have made my lot secure." "You will not abandon me to the realm of the dead, nor will you let me see decay." "You make known to me the path of life, you fill me with joy in your presence, with eternal pleasures at your right hand." That "you" is our Lord and Savior. A very particular, specific Savior indeed. This very particular human Savior with dirt under his fingernails and aching feet like us, who got frustrated and angry just like we do, reaches across time to us, to very specific and particular individuals and says: "Come with me. Find your rest and your salvation with me. I'm the one you've been waiting for."

Because we look to a very specific and particular Savior, we find the hope that he speaks to us as specific and particular individuals. Jesus knows what it is to be an individual in the midst of human history and daily life, Jesus knows what it is to reach the end of the day tired and weary, Jesus knows what it is to deal with people who don't listen, who aren't paying any attention to you, who overlook you, don't seem to understand you, Jesus knows all about what it is to be where you are. And our salvation comes through him and only through him. That's the message that Peter was preaching to those people in Jerusalem that day, and to us: "Your salvation has come, and I can tell you through whom and by whom – Jesus of Nazareth."

This man, this Jesus, this specific, particular person, who was born, who lived, who died, who lives again and forever, came to save you.

And to save every other specific, particular person who has ever, or will ever, live, as well.

Amen.

The Known Unknown
John 14:15-21; Acts 17:22-31

May 29, 2011

I want to begin by considering Paul there in Athens, because it is an interesting moment in the Book of Acts. Here is Paul venturing into very different territory than he has been in before. Athens was a city focused on education and learning. Greek philosophy had been around for centuries and people enjoyed thinking and debating and arguing about all sorts of issues and ideas. The people of Athens were cosmopolitan, they were intellectual, they were curious.

But Paul was not initially welcomed with open arms there in Athens - his reputation was as a religious leader, more a zealot than a theologian. So he was coming into what we might call "enemy territory," especially now that he was an evangelist for the emerging Christian Church. He was going up against this reputation of the Athenians: intellectual, curious, political, argumentative, and not set on any one religion or god, "spiritual but not religious".

The Athenians worshiped many gods, and not just the familiar gods of Greek mythology like Zeus and Apollo and Athena, from whom Athens got its name, but they worshiped different gods for almost every aspect of life. There was a god you prayed to when you mowed your lawn, and a god you prayed to whenever you planted tomatoes, and a god for safe travel, and a god for success in business—a god for every aspect of daily life. Paul noticed on every corner, shrines and idols set up to these various gods. One particular shrine caught his eye, that's the one he mentions in today's reading as he is speaking before the Areopagus, the advisory council of Athens. Paul says: "I've noticed that you Athenians are very religious, very spiritual, you have all these shrines on every street corner, and

I noticed one that said: TO AN UNKNOWN GOD. Well now, today, right here, the God you have been worshipping as unknown, I proclaim to you. Let me tell you about the God that up until now to you has been unknown." And Paul goes on to tell them about Jesus.

This story raises some interesting questions, especially in our modern world. Are we like these Athenians? Do we worship an unknown God? Is our God unknown?

This gets us to one of the deep paradoxes of our faith. God is the Creator of everything and we can't even begin to get our minds wrapped around that. God is mysterious and awesome and powerful. Omnipotent. Omnipresent. All those "omni" descriptions trying to put into words the fact that God is "all" things at "all" times. All-Knowing. All-Seeing. All-Powerful. We humans have no way to even begin to grasp the power of God and the working of God's mind, God's will, God's wisdom. God is awesome and mysterious. No one has ever seen God, truly, not even Moses who, though he "talked to God face-to-face," when he asked God for the chance to see God, God told him "no one can see me and live," and only allowed Moses to glimpse God's backside.

And yet...our God is not entirely unknown. God has made himself knowable to us through the prophets, through Scripture, through our own spiritual experiences, through other people, and especially and most clearly through Jesus Christ. Our unknown God became known to us by becoming human and living among us as one of us, while also remaining divine. So if you ask me: "What does God look like?" I would have to admit: "I have no idea." But if you ask me: "What is God like?" ah, that I can begin to answer.

God is like a mother with her infant child in her arms. God is like a father caring for his children, maybe even at times carrying them, piggyback, when they are too tired to walk on their own. God is like a mother hen, protecting her chicks by spreading her wings over them. God is like a shepherd, like a shady spot on a hot summer's day, like a refreshing drink of water in the middle of the desert. Scripture is full of images of what God is like, and above all, God is like Jesus.

Jesus said: "Whoever knows me, knows my Father." To know Jesus is to know God, or at least to begin to know what God is like. So we can know that, like Jesus, God is compassionate and merciful and caring, like Jesus God is with us. Notice that is also what Paul says, that even as we are searching, groping for God, perhaps feeling like we are in the dark, God is right there with us, not far from any of us. Paul goes on to remind us that God is not like the things of this world, God is not like gold or silver or stone or any commodity or any of the stuff of this world. God does not wear out or wear down or rust or rot away or lose value over time. That is why we should resist the temptation to worship such idols, earthly things in place of God. God is always much larger, more durable, more powerful, more secure than anything we can find or imagine in this life. So we do know, to some degree, what God is like...sometimes by knowing what God is not like, in the negative. God is like Jesus but not like any of the idols of this world.

Our unknown God is no longer entirely unknown, not here in the wake of Easter. Now we can know God. That's pretty amazing–it still remains a paradox, of course–that this unknowable God of ours, the Creator of everything, beyond anything we can ever begin to imagine, can be known by us, at least as well as we need to know on this side of Paradise. Known through Jesus and known through love.

Jesus says: "Those who love me and keep my commandments will now me and through me will know God." What was the main commandment Jesus gave us? To love: to love God and each other. So that's the equation for knowing God: The more we love, the more we know Christ, and the more we know

21

Christ, the more we know God. God is revealed through Jesus and through love.

Of course it sounds so simple put that way. And it is. Simple, but far from easy. It is in fact the most difficult thing in the world to do. And this is a lifelong learning experience. That's why we keep gathering for worship. That's why we keep praying, keep reading and returning to Scripture – because there is always more to learn about love and how to do it and do it consistently and do it well, from the heart. If any of you think you love perfectly already, you are excused from the rest of the sermon.

(Pause)

Let the record show no one got up and left.

It takes a lifetime, at least, to learn how to love and to put it into practice every moment of every day. By continuing to learn about and practice love, we continue to learn about Jesus. And by continuing to do those things, we continue to get to know God better and better – not perfectly, but better. There's always more to learn about love and about Jesus, and therefore about God. And yet God continues to surprise and amaze us. God can be known but God always remains unknown– mysterious and surprising and amazing and unexpected. Just when we think we have God all figured out, God does something to remind us how little we really know. This is not unlike human relationships. In marriage and in other deep relationships, we never have the other person all figured out, there's always more to discover about people, even people we've known all our lives or been married to for 70 years. Love requires time and intimacy and communication and connection.

If God remains in our minds an abstract, distant, cold, theological concept, we will never truly be able to love God.

But God is not abstract and distant and cold, God is always right here with us, walking with us, showering us with love. God is not a divine watchmaker who winds up the universe and then just sits back and lets it go, watching at a distance. God is always right here with us, in the midst of daily life, and knowing that we can start loving God and loving God more we can begin to know God more. Not in theological treatises but in our everyday lives and experiences, and in our hearts. And that's how our journey of faith progresses.

It is all wrapped up with love - love for each other and love for God - and as we keep working on that everything else begins to fall into place. There's always more to learn and always a way to do better, each day.

The Athenians, Paul saw, had an inclination towards the spiritual. They were, though, in his mind, wasting that spiritual inclination by worshiping gods they made with their own hands, gods that could literally be put in a box. Small gods, limited gods. So Paul tries to convince them to seek out and search for the true God, the huge, unlimited God that Paul knew. The Creator, the Savior. The God who is not just in charge of one small aspect of your life, not just the god who has control over how well your corn grows or whether you'll find a parking space, but the God who is in control of everything. One God, no need for multiple shrines. Don't settle for small gods. Seek for the one, true God. The only one you need.

This is also Paul's message to us, acknowledging the spiritual inclination that I believe all humans feel to some degree. We all want to know some answers, to find some purpose larger than ourselves, to love and be loved, to find a foundation on which to build our lives. Paul speaks across the ages to us: "Keep looking, keep learning, but don't waste that effort on small, human-made gods and idols, keep seeking out the true God, the God of love, the God revealed in Jesus."

And ever since Jesus walked this earth and lived among us, ever since he taught and healed and laughed and wept and died and rose again, ever since then our unknown God has no longer been unknown. Not entirely. This we proclaim.

Amen.

War Weary

Matthew 11:16-19, 25-30; Romans 7:15-25a

July 3, 2011

Last week when we read from an earlier chapter in Romans, I suggested that what Paul is telling us is that we have a choice: we can be slaves to this world or slaves to God's kingdom. Of course Paul is encouraging us to be the latter, to be slaves in the sense of obeying and following God's law, for it is only in doing so that we find true freedom. That's where I left things last Sunday.

Today I want to start with that idea - that in God we find our true freedom. Tomorrow is Independence Day, so it seems a good time to be discussing freedom. One important question which I think needs to be asked when talking about freedom is: "freedom from what?"

On July 4, 1776, we as a nation declared our freedom from Great Britain, our freedom from "taxation without representation," our freedom from tyranny, at least the tyranny from across the sea.

As we consider the freedom we find in God, what is it we are declaring freedom from? Paul says the freedom that we find in God is freedom from sin. Not from sinning itself, but from the struggle against sin and the effects of sin, the guilt and anxiety that result from our struggle against sin. Paul compares this struggle to a war, a civil war within each of us that we fight every day, a war within us between Spirit and Flesh, as Paul describes it. And by "flesh" Paul doesn't just mean our bodies, but our lower, baser instincts. The civil war between sin and that divine spark, that imago Dei, that image of God, within us. There is a war raging in each of us, every day, between sin and what Abraham Lincoln called the "better angels of our nature."

Knowing what to do is not the problem. Doing it is the problem. Here's how Paul describes it: *"I do not understand my own actions. For I do not do what I want, but I do the very thing I hate…I can will what is right, but I cannot do it. For I do not do the good I want, but the evil I do not want is what I do…I see in my members another law at war with the law of my mind, making me captive to the law of sin…Wretched man that I am!"* Remember, this is the apostle Paul talking, someone I would put near the top of the list of those who truly lived a Christian life, at least after his experience on the Road to Damascus. Even Paul had trouble doing the right thing sometimes.

The good I want to do I do not do, instead I do the very opposite. I know what I should do, I know perhaps even what God wants me to do, but I can't do it. I just can't. I want to, I really do, but I can't. I know what I shouldn't do, I even resolve not to do that, but that is the very thing I find myself doing, almost despite myself.

Any of this sound familiar to anybody?

"I'm not going to eat that last piece of pie. I'm not going to do it." And then suddenly it's 3 o'clock in the morning and you find yourself opening the refrigerator, reaching for that piece of pie.

"I'm going to read the Bible, every morning." But then, darn that snooze alarm, you hit it and get another ten minutes of sleep and it feels so warm and cozy there in bed, and by the time you do get up you're rushing just to make it to work on time. "I'll read the Bible later, when I have time."

"I'm going to exercise every single day, I'm going to force myself to go outside and walk, every day." Well, it's a little chilly out there today, and there's a threat of rain. Maybe tomorrow. For today I'll just grab some Doritos and sit by the TV.

We are human. Even Paul was human, believe it or not. Even Paul is experiencing this: "I know what I should do but I can't quite do it. I know what I shouldn't be doing and that is the very thing I find myself doing."

Here's how John Calvin wrote about this passage in Romans and about this war-like struggle within each of us: *"The godly…in whom the regeneration of God is begun, are so divided, that with the chief desire of the heart they aspire to God, seek celestial righteousness, hate sin, and yet they are drawn down to the earth by the relics of their flesh: and thus, while pulled in two ways, they fight against their own nature, and nature fights against them…this is the Christian conflict between the flesh and the spirit."*

Now Martin Luther comes at the passage and the struggle from a slightly different perspective, as one might expect: *"The saints are at the same time sinners while they are righteous. They are righteous, because they believe in Christ…but they are sinners, inasmuch as they do not fulfill the Law, and still have sinful lusts. They are like sick people who are being treated by a physician. They are really sick, but hope and are beginning to get, or be made, well. They are about to regain their health. Such patients would suffer the greatest harm by arrogantly claiming to be well, for they would suffer a relapse that is worse than their first illness."*

John Calvin says it is a war within, a battle; Martin Luther says we're sin-sick souls.

Paul reminds us that this battle, this sickness is exhausting. When soldiers fight in a physical war, they often develop mental scars, which over the years we have called "battle fatigue" or "Post-Traumatic-Stress-Disorder." I think Paul is suggesting, in a very different context of course, that we all spiritually suffer from "battle fatigue." It is exhausting and fatiguing to fight against sin and its pull, to fight against our very selves in our hearts and our minds. The awareness of our own sin is frustrating, it's exhausting.

Don't you sometimes wish you weren't a Christian, that you didn't have to worry about this? If you didn't care about any of this sin stuff, if you didn't care about trying to live up to God's expectations, you wouldn't have this battle inside, at least not to this degree. You'd just do whatever you wanted, no questions asked, no guilt, no shame. That's some people's definition of freedom: just do whatever you want. But as Christians, as those who are trying to obey God and follow the teachings and the example of Jesus Christ, we enter into this war, this struggle. What Would Jesus Do? Well, he probably wouldn't do a lot of the things we do, we know that.

Who among us isn't a little war weary, fatigued by that battle? I'm trying, but...I seem to take one step forward, two steps back. The spirit is willing, but the flesh is weak. O wretched man that I am.

But Paul doesn't leave us there. Don't miss what Paul says next: "Who will rescue me from this body of death? Thanks be to God through Jesus Christ our Lord!" There's hope. Hope of begin rescued from this struggle. God will rescue you. Jesus will rescue you. That's what Jesus himself says at the end of today's passage from Matthew's Gospel. He says: "Hey, you there - war weary and sin-sick. Come to me, all of you who are weary and carrying heavy burdens and fighting seemingly impossible battles and struggling against sin in your own life, and I will give you rest. I'm gentle and humble in heart, and in me you will find rest for your souls." Rest from your battle, rest from your struggle, rest for your sin-sick soul.

Know that you are loved and forgiven despite your personal losing battle against sin. Know that the Lord will provide the strength and courage you need for that battle and the relief you need from it. Know that you have relief from the guilt and the anxiety that is a part of that battle. Know that you can say: "Lord, take this burden from me. I struggle, and I need some rest. So take this from me, Lord." And he will.

I think that's why Martin Luther famously once declared in a letter: "Be a sinner and sin boldly." He didn't mean go against God, but he meant go out and live your life and struggle and do it boldly knowing that God is with you and that God will give you the relief and the rest that you need in the midst of your battles. That's why Luther goes on in that quote to say: "but believe and rejoice in Christ even more boldly." We have a Great Physician who can and will heal us from whatever ails us. "There is a balm in Gilead to soothe the sin-sick soul." That is where our true freedom lies, and what it is freedom from. The freedom not to be done with the battle, but to find relief and renewed strength and courage in the midst of the on-going battle, so that we always live to fight another day. Relief from the guilt and shame of always falling short of what God expects or what we expect, knowing that God will be right there to pick us up and dust us off and give us another opportunity. That is true freedom. Not doing whatever we want, but doing, as best we can, what God wants, again and again and again.

And so I remind you, with some help from Paul and Calvin and Luther, about true freedom. Freedom from sin, or at least from the worst effects of the struggle against sin. And that freedom is found in one place, in one person, in Jesus Christ.

Happy Independence Day!

Amen.

II. More Recent Ramblings

Goings-On in Bethlehem
Micah 5:2-5; Luke 1:46-55

4th Sunday of Advent
December 23, 2018

We conclude this season of Advent with two fairly familiar readings, which reminds me that one of the problems with such familiar readings is we can get so used to hearing them each year that we miss what they are really saying. These are two pretty radical passages of Scripture, particularly Mary's words in the Magnificat, although the newer translation we read just now did not use the phrase "magnify the Lord" but had Mary saying her soul "glorifies the Lord." I am reminding you this morning of the radical nature of these familiar readings because they point us to the radical nature of the birth we will be celebrating in the next week.

First, a word or two about the situation at the time of the prophet Micah. It is thought that Micah was prophesying sometime in the 8th century B.C. This was a time of particular turmoil in the region that we now call "Israel," although I would remind you, by this time in the history of the Hebrew people, the kingdom had split in two. The northern kingdom of Israel had been invaded by the Assyrian empire and the Assyrians had gotten all the way to the gates of Jerusalem but had not managed to invade or take over the city itself, and although they had pulled back a bit, the northern half of the kingdom known as Israel is now gone, now under Assyrian rule. The southern kingdom of Judah is still feeling particularly anxious and vulnerable – they have staved off danger, but for how long? This is a time when the people are fearful, they see danger all around them, especially from the Assyrians, but there are also indications of the Babylonian empire growing in their part of the world as well, so it's a time when the people of Judah are feeling very anxious about forces just beyond that seem out of their control, yet which they fear might destroy them eventually. Hmmmm, feeling like the world is out of control, certainly out of our control...

Does that sound at all familiar?

There is also some worry in Judah because there have been a lot of refugees streaming south from that northern kingdom of Israel since they have been invaded and there is growing concern about these extra people, concern that they may, for one thing, be bringing Assyrians with them, concerns that they may stretch the resources of Judah too thin: "Can we take in all these people?" Hmmm, concern about refugees and migrants...

Does that sound at all familiar?

Also at this time with these concerns and worries about outside dangers, the people of Judah are not particularly confident in their own leaders at this time. Their leaders have been shown to be corrupt and out for their own gain, not for the good of the people. In fact part of what has been done to keep the Assyrians at bay is the rulers of Judah have said we will pay the Assyrians tribute money to stay away, and this money is not coming out of the pocket of the rulers; they are getting it from the pockets of the poor by increased taxes. Hmmmm, leaders that seem corrupt and in whom the people have lost faith...

Does that sound familiar at all?

And finally, the society of Judah is splintering, as the small segment of those who are in control and rich are getting richer and the rest of the population, especially the poor and the needy, seem to be getting poorer.

Does this sound familiar at all?

So the people of Judah in this time period feel beset by forces without and within, and it is into this situation that Micah steps and begins to prophesy. And notice that today, here in this passage, his message is: Help is coming. But don't look to the seat of government in Jerusalem to expect a leader to arise to solve our problems. No, Micah says look to Bethlehem, this little out-of-the-way place. That's where our help will come from, Micah declares: a great ruler will arise out of this seemingly insignificant place, a ruler who will shepherd his people and care for them rather than for himself. A ruler who will care for his people and serve them and bring peace. Not a peace that comes from paying tribute, not a peace that comes from building walls and fortresses, but a peace that comes from ruling and living the way God wants a ruler to act. Don't lose hope, Micah is saying, but also don't look in the usual places – God rarely, if ever, acts the way we humans expect, or in the places where we expect God to act. And of course we, here, so many centuries later, as Christians, look to this prophecy and believe Micah is talking about Jesus. "She who is in labor will give birth" to a true Savior, not of this world but of God's kingdom.

This leads us naturally to Mary, the totally unexpected mother of this Savior. This young woman without many real-world prospects except marriage - and she's not even married yet. And the angel Gabriel appears to her and declares: "You are about to bear a child." I think it is safe to say that Mary probably felt some anxiety at hearing those words, but very quickly, at least according to Luke, she responds: "let it be with me according to your word."

Mary who then journeys to visit her cousin Elizabeth - old and barren but also miraculously pregnant with a child herself. The two rejoice together and Mary bursts into signing, singing this great song of praise. But notice this is a radical song declaring what is coming with the birth of her child. I find it particularly interesting that many of the themes that Mary lifts up in her song are themes that Jesus himself will lift up and preach about in his ministry.

Mary says first of all "I rejoice that God has looked upon someone so small and insignificant as me. I rejoice that God has lifted me, even me, up to be highly favored." And then she goes on to remind us that the birth of this child, this King, this Savior, is going to turn everything upside down, not just her own life, but the entire world—past, present, and future. Nothing will ever be the same.

Mary points us to the fact that this Savior who is coming will himself lift up the lowly and bring down the proud and the powerful. We Christians, I fear, have too often boiled down this birth and this season to Hallmark card status—a quaint little hillside with a clean stable and animals that don't smell at all or shed or make noise, and a happy couple with no doubts or fears and this baby with no crying or diapers to change, but Mary will not let us forget the radical and real-life nature of what is about to happen. The One who is coming, the One she is bearing in her womb will begin setting things right, and that might be good news or not-so- good news depending on your position along the spectrum of power and prosperity and prominence currently. Jesus comes to lift up the poor, the oppressed, the outcast, the lowly, the overlooked. Jesus comes to raise up all those that human society so often beats down and keeps down. But the reverse is also true: Jesus comes to bring down those who are proud and arrogant and powerful and rich already and not sharing their resources and blessings or paying attention to those in need, all those in that first category. Jesus comes to feed the hungry but to also remind those who are full about the reality of hunger.

To many in this world, all this is good news. But to some of us who are already rich and powerful and privileged in the scheme of things, this "good news" might give us pause. Knowing what is coming, and all this is still in process, might make us want to be sure we jump on board God's train before it runs us over.

Lifting up the poor and the hungry and the oppressed and the outcast and bringing down the rich and the powerful and the proud doesn't fit so neatly or sound so good on a Hallmark card. But that is the real meaning of this season and this birth. That should give us pause – it doesn't mean we won't rejoice, but it might make us consider our behavior, our position, our status right now.

The bottom line in all of this is a reminder, a simple but profound reminder, that as we end this season of Advent and prepare ourselves to be ready for the birth of this child, this King, this Savior, we should ponder how we are going to react and behave in response. The reminder that Christmas is coming whether we like it or not. That means change is coming - nothing will ever be the same, we cannot stay the same.

Ready or not, here it comes.

Amen.

Like Trees

Jeremiah 17:5-10; Psalm 1

February 17, 2019

I think that I shall never see a sermon lovely as a tree.

I've always liked trees. I can remember specific favorite trees from my childhood: the maple tree right outside my window in our front yard and the sound the wind would make through its leaves; the buckeye tree that grew outside the cafeteria at my junior high school and the rush to try to get one of the buckeyes that fell from that tree in autumn. Even now I love being around trees, one of the things that attracted me to my house here was all the trees around it, and the fact I can sit on my deck and be up in the trees, surrounded by them, like good friends.

Trees are majestic and elegant and strong, and I love the different sounds the wind makes in the leaves of different trees – cottonwoods, I think, are my favorite. Trees bend with that wind, they send down deep roots, they provide shade and beauty. There is a lot to love and admire about trees, which is one reason I hate to see those logging trucks we see so often around here, and I mourn for those trees that get cut down.

I suppose my love of trees is also one of the reasons I've always liked both of today's passages of Scripture, remarkable similar both in their message and their language: both use the image of a tree to describe those who trust in God. "Those who trust in God are truly happy, they are like trees, planted by streams of water," sending their roots deep, rooted in God, nourished by the sun, watered by God's Word. What a rich, beautiful, comforting image, which I also find very calming...like sitting underneath a tree.

Both these readings are essentially giving us the choice: we can trust God and be like a calm…strong…deeply rooted…well-fed tree - or we can be frenetic and chaotic and blown every which way and be rushing here and there always stressed and anxious; unfortunately I think our entire world is more like that these days than like the calm, serene, rooted tree. People seem very anxious these days, many people always running, always distracted, rushing from one item on their busy schedule to the next with no time for reflection or even a deep, calming breath. And we have these electronic devices now that we carry around as if they were part of our bodies, and which keep distracting us from life and from each other, pulling us away from real connection. We have substances – drugs, alcohol, sugar, fast food – that we use almost distractedly, without thinking, and which we need more and more of to get the same distraction. We live in a world that doesn't seem very satisfied, a world full of people who don't seem very rooted or secure at all. Everything seems uncertain, up-in-the-air, disconcerting, disconnected.

Jeremiah declares that those who trust in themselves rather than God are like a shrub that is dry, parched, brittle, prickly with thorns. And when the wind blows, those desert shrubs are not going to hold on very long, they become tumble weeds. How many of us are like tumbleweeds, just rolling constantly wherever the winds blow us? Psalm 1 says that those who do not trust God are like dust, something else that just gets blown about by the wind. Both the tumbleweed and the dust are contrasted with the tree, which remains rooted in place; even in times of drought finding nourishment; even in storms standing firm, bending perhaps but not breaking. A powerful contrast of imagery, which gets to the heart of the effects of trusting in God or trusting in oneself alone.

Thomas Merton wrote, in a wonderful book aptly titled <u>New Seeds of Contemplation</u>: *"A tree gives glory to God by being a tree. For in being what God means it to be it is obeying [God]…The more a tree is like itself, the more it is like [God]. If it tried to be like something else which it was never intended to be, it would be less like God and therefore it would give [God] less glory.*" A tree is a tree. A rose is a rose is a rose. Part of what trees teach us is to be who we are, who God made us to be. Another troubling aspect of our modern world, in my opinion, is that so many people seem to be trying to change their appearance, change who they seem to be, change what people think of them. That is part of the allure of social media, to present yourself to the world the way you want to be seen, not necessarily the way you are. We live in a world in which many people are always trying to be something else other than what they are - that can be a good thing if people are striving to be better, to be more loving, but I fear most of the time this is more about the surface than what's underneath. And this reveals an underlying discomfort and dissatisfaction among so many with who they are – with their body, with their lives, always wanting to look different or even to be different than who they are.

But it would be ridiculous for an apple tree to be disappointed that it couldn't produce peaches. That would be like the situation the apostle Paul describes of an eye wanting to be a hand or an ear wanting to be a foot, of parts of the body wishing they were some other part. Pauls' point is that we all come together as separate people with distinct gifts and talents to make one body, the body of Christ, and to be more than the sum of our parts. But that requires us to do our part, not try to do someone else's, or regret what we cannot do rather than enjoying what we can do. We each have our identity, our God-given identity. Perhaps trees can teach us to be who we are.

Also notice both of today's readings talk not just about trusting in God but being nourished by God's Word. That is where happiness and contentment are found. Not in the human rat race, not in trying to acquire more things, but in trusting God and trying to align our lives with God's Word. I'm reminded of the song "If I Were a Rich Man" from the musical *Fiddler on the Roof* which the main character, Tevye, sings. The song is about him wanting money, primarily, but at one point in that song he also sings: *"If I were rich, I'd have the time that I lack to sit in the synagogue and pray and maybe have a seat by the Eastern wall. And I'd discuss the holy books with the learned men, several hours every day and that would be the sweetest thing of all (sigh)."* What Tevye really longs for is the time to rest in God's presence and feed on God's word – that is worth more than all the money in the world.

One final lesson for us from the tree – both today's readings talk about bearing fruit. We all are called to bear fruit, but we don't all bear the same kind of fruit, nor do we all bear fruit at the same time or at the same speed. Our growing seasons are all different. That is a particularly good lesson for us as a community of faith. We are not all apple trees or cherry trees or fig trees or olive trees, we are not all preachers or teachers or evangelists or musicians. We bring with us a variety of fruit, a variety of talents and skills and gifts. We shouldn't expect everyone in a community of faith to be producing fruit at the same time or in the same way. Each tree produces its own unique fruit or flower or nut or leaf, and they do so at different times of the year, and so it is with us, as followers of Christ, as members of the body of Christ together. The important point is for us to stay together and to stay rooted in God's Word and in God's promises, calm and confident, working and worshipping together.

So let's keep this image of a tree in mind and be confident we each are rooted here and now, right where we are supposed to be at this moment, called together as a diverse forest of different types of trees, each bearing its own unique type of fruit. Like trees, let's keep trusting that, even if we encounter times of drought, or some stormy weather along the way, we will, together, bear fruit, each in our own way, in God's time.

Amen.

41

How Easter Changes Lives – Part One
Revelation 1:4-8; Acts 5:27-32

2nd Sunday of Easter
April 28, 2019

There's an old story – the version I saw recently is thought to come from the Orient – of a general and his marauding army going through the countryside. As they entered a small village one day, the general called his scouts and asked: "How many people are in this village?" The scouts replied that all the villagers had fled except for the town's priest who was still in the temple. The general asked: "Well who is going to pay tribute then?" He stormed into the temple, and found the priest quietly praying. The general shouted: "Stand up! Don't you know that I am the one who can run you through without batting an eye?" The old priest quietly replied: "Don't you know that I am the one who can be run through without batting an eye?" The general stood there for a moment in disbelief, and then a smile danced on his lips. He bowed and left the temple, leaving the priest to his prayers.

I was reminded of that story because of both of our readings for this Easter Sunday, especially the passage from Acts. Let me remind you where we left Peter last week at the end of Luke's account of the Easter story. We left Peter after first not believing the women's account about seeing Jesus alive and risen, then running to the tomb and seeing it empty for himself, and finally leaving the tomb and going home wondering what exactly had happened. So we left him wondering and uncertain.

Now we jump ahead to the events described in the 3rd, 4th, and 5th chapters of Acts, which begin with Peter encountering a lame beggar in Jerusalem. The beggar, of course, asks for "alms," for some sort of financial assistance, and Peter replies to him: "I'm not going to give you gold or silver, I don't have those to give – and, that's not really what you need anyway – but, in the name of Jesus Christ, stand up and walk." The beggar does; he is instantly healed. And, as we might say nowadays, "the crowd went wild." Everyone is amazed at this display of healing power, and the news gets back to the religious leaders, who probably had their spies out in the crowd that day anyway. These are the same religious leaders who had condemned Jesus not too long before and demanded his crucifixion. They round up Peter and John and bring them before the council, during which time they demand that the disciples stop healing people in the name of Jesus, stop preaching about Jesus, and really just stop talking about Jesus to anyone, ever again. The council accuses them of being "disruptive."

Of course Peter and John don't follow any of these demands. They leave the council and immediately go back to doing what they have been doing – healing and preaching and teaching about Jesus. In fact, we are told by Luke that the number of believers is growing, and they are praying for "boldness." They are acting so bold that the council leaders have Peter and some other disciples thrown in jail. And the very first night they are in jail the doors are all opened by an angel who tells them to go back to the Temple and keep on preaching and teaching about Jesus, which they do. Now the leaders of the council get wind of this as well and when they investigate they discover that the jail doors are all locked (*the angel must have locked them back up after letting the disciples go – those sneaky angels!*) and yet Peter and the disciples are gone. Now it is the religious leaders who start "wondering." Then someone tells them: "Hey, those guys you threw in jail are back in the Temple teaching about Jesus," and that's when the council has them brought back before them, which brings us to the beginning of today's passage.

At this point the council is ever angrier than they were before because in addition to the disciples preaching and teaching and being "disruptive," now they are also boldly and deliberately disobeying the demands of the council. And nothing makes puffed up, insecure, authoritarian leaders angrier than being disobeyed and made to look foolish. That's why in today's reading the council erupts at the disciples: "How dare you! We demand, we double-dare demand, that you stop doing this...oh, and by the way, stop saying that we are the ones who killed Jesus, too." And Peter looks them squarely in the eye, these authorities who helped kill Jesus, and says to them: "We must obey God...not you."

Remember - this is Peter. This is Peter who just a few months earlier out in the courtyard of this very same council couldn't even muster the courage to step inside the council chambers the night Jesus was arrested and hauled before them - Peter, out in the courtyard, who was confronted by a servant girl who asked: "Aren't you one of that Jesus guy's followers?" and Peter denied – not once, not twice, but three separate times – that he even knew who Jesus was. Now Peter is standing before the very same council, face-to-face, and telling them in uncertain terms that he must follow Jesus and not them; denying not Jesus this time, but them.

How does a person change like that? How does that happen? Peter has undergone a pretty radical change. I have always thought that one of the best pieces of evidence – if you are looking for evidence – for the factual truth of the resurrection of Jesus Christ is the radical change in his followers after that event. The followers who, like Peter, on that first Easter Sunday were fearful and disheartened and cowering in fear and wondering what had happened – within days and weeks were boldly proclaiming Jesus as the risen Lord, teaching in Jesus' name, and even saying to the religious and political authorities of their day: "We don't care what you say or what you threaten to do to us. Bring it on. We're with Jesus Christ." That sort of transformation doesn't happen because of a mere myth or fairy tale or lie. These are people who experienced something that transformed them from cowering disciples into bold evangelists. As Peter tells the council: "We have seen Jesus – I have seen him. I saw him die, and I have seen the empty tomb. I have even seen the risen Lord. I've touched his hands and feet. I've eaten breakfast with him – a breakfast Jesus himself prepared with his own hands for me – he is alive! And knowing that Jesus is alive, I also know that there's nothing you earthly authorities can do to me." Peter might well have added: "Don't you know that I am the one who can be run through without batting an eye?"

Something pretty amazing has to happen to change someone that drastically. And something pretty amazing did. Jesus rose from the dead. Jesus is alive! Death has lost its sting. "I know that my Redeemer lives." That is life-changing – world-changing. That's Easter. It can change the most fearful, cowering figure into a bold proclaimer of faith.

I think that's also what we glimpse in the beginning of the Book of Revelation. This book is written much later than Acts, and although attributed to the disciple named John, most scholars would agree that we really don't know for sure who wrote it, but it is someone writing at the end of the first century A.D. By this time, decades after the earthly life of Jesus, there had been enough time for the Church to grow but for intense opposition to the Church to also grow. This was a time of increasing persecution against some of the early Christians by the Roman Empire. Despite that, here we have this person writing a letter to the churches in Asia that is surely going to get passed around – writing bold words about Jesus in this climate of potential persecution and opposition. Jesus: the Alpha and the Omega; the one who is and was and is coming again; the firstborn of the dead; the ruler of all the kings of the earth – these are bold words even today but especially in the climate of the late first century A.D. These are words that, if they had been brought to the attention of certain rulers and kings, could have caused real harm for the person who wrote them, perhaps even death. But this person sent them out into the world to be read by anyone who wanted to read them. This is someone else who has experienced the emboldening power of Easter – I know Jesus is alive, so I do not fear any earthly power or authority. "Don't you know that I am the one who can be run through without batting an eye?"

That's the transforming power of Easter - the power of not just the empty tomb but an encounter with our risen Lord in some way. The power that, when things look dark and lost and hopeless, can turn it all around in an instant, and with no rational explanation, not through anything we do. Easter transforms lives. Easter brings life anew to what seemed dead and lifeless. It can transform our world. It can even transform us - here and now, today.

That is such good news that we're going to continue considering it next week when we read perhaps the greatest example in Scripture of how an encounter with the risen Lord can transform someone. We will consider the story of how one of the greatest enemies of the early Church was turned into one of the greatest messengers of that same Church. The story of a guy named Saul.

Amen.

How Easter Changes Lives – Part Two"
John 21:15-19; Acts 9:1-20

3rd Sunday of Easter
May 5, 2019

Today I continue reflecting on the impact of Easter on people in Scripture and hopefully on us, too – the impact of encountering the risen Lord and knowing that Jesus is alive.

I included in our readings today this short passage about Peter because I have been talking about him the past two Sundays and I wanted to acknowledge this moment in John's Gospel. Peter and the other disciples have been out in their boats without catching any fish – they have gone back to Galilee and their fishing boats for some reason – when Jesus appears to them again there on the beach. They don't recognize him – again for reasons that are unclear since they have already encountered him resurrected back in Jerusalem – but he advises them to throw their nets off the other side of the boat and they do that and suddenly their nets are full of an abundance of fish, so they know this man is Jesus. Peter impetuously – Peter never did anything half-way – jumps into the water and swims to shore, where Jesus has prepared breakfast for them. Then Peter and Jesus have this conversation recorded in John 21.

I think it is pretty clear why Jesus asks Peter three separate times: "Do you love me?" It is a reversal of the three-fold denial that Peter offered on the night Jesus was betrayed and arrested, when Peter denied three times that he even knew who Jesus was. But I was thinking about it again in the context of the impact of Easter on people's lives, and realizing that Jesus doesn't ask these questions of Peter because Jesus doesn't know the answer – I mean, as Peter says to Jesus: "You know everything, Lord; you know I love you" – Jesus knows that

Peter loves him. I'm convinced Jesus asks Peter these questions solely for Peter's benefit. It's a three-fold counteracting of his three-fold denial – for every time Peter said publicly: "I don't know Jesus," Jesus now gives him the opportunity to publicly declare: "I love Jesus." For Peter's benefit. Have you ever done something to someone, maybe especially unintentionally, and what you then most want to do is make it up to them...somehow? Well Jesus is giving Peter that chance – that chance to say to Jesus, face-to-face: "I'm sorry. I love you. You know I love you." I don't think up until this point Peter had really processed - intellectually and emotionally - his denial of Jesus. I suspect, given what we know about Peter, that he hadn't taken a lot of soul-searching time to really deal with the fact that he had denied – three times – the most important person in his life. So Jesus allows him to do that here – I wonder if that is why we are told that Peter was feeling sad, particularly by the third time he answered – maybe it was beginning to sink in to him: "I did deny Jesus, but I still love him." This is a way for Peter to acknowledge to himself "I love Jesus...despite my denial." Peter has already been forgiven by Jesus for that three-fold denial (after all Jesus said from the cross: "Father, forgive them, they know not what they do") and now Peter has to learn how to forgive himself. Jesus offers him at least the beginning of that opportunity here. This is a reminder, I think, that part of the power of Easter is allowing us to move beyond the past, to move beyond past mistakes and past sins. Easter reminds us that we are not just loved by God but forgiven - forgiven for all past sins and mistakes and regrets. But we have to acknowledge that for ourselves to make it truly real for ourselves.

Talking about being forgiven for your past is perhaps the perfect transition to the story of Paul, or Saul as he is still known in today's reading. If there's anyone in the Bible who because of their past should be disqualified from being a follower of Christ, it's Saul - as he himself readily acknowledges in some of his letters. He may not have killed Christians himself, but he has certainly arranged for it to happen, not to mention stood by holding people's coats while they stoned Stephen. Saul has made it his mission to disrupt and persecute the early Church. As today's passage begins, he is going to Damascus "spewing murderous schemes," planning to go arrest and kill even more Christians, but then…literally…he sees the light. He has this incident on the road to Damascus when he sees a bright light and is blinded - and I always picture him falling off his horse although the Bible doesn't say that. Saul has a conversation with - his own personal encounter with - the risen Lord. He hears the voice of Jesus asking him: "Saul, why do you persecute me?"

"Who are you, Lord?"

"I am Jesus of Nazareth – you know, the guy whose followers you've been persecuting. Now go to Damascus and await further instructions."

I feel almost sorry for Saul here, but the person in this story I really feel sorry for is Ananias. I mean, Saul deserves to be blinded after what he has done to these early Christians, but Ananias is a good, devoted, faithful follower of Jesus. Ananias also receives a message from Jesus in a vision - another encounter with the risen Lord - and I'm sure Ananias was excited and really eager to hear what Jesus had to tell him, but Jesus says: "Ananias, there's this guy in town named Saul of Tarsus, and I want you to go find him – he already knows you're coming – go there, lay hands on him and give him his sight back." And Ananias, understandably, answers back: "Um…Lord…are you serious? Do you know who this guy Saul is? I've heard all about this guy – he's not a nice guy, Lord! In fact, he's an enemy of your followers and of you!"

And Jesus says: "I know…I know all about this Saul of Tarsus. Trust me. Go see him. I know what I'm doing. Saul has been chosen to be an instrument, and agent, for me and the

Church." Jesus even adds: "Don't worry. Saul will suffer a bit along the way that has been chosen for him."

So Ananias goes. He does everything Jesus asks him to do – he lays hands on Saul and restores his sight. Saul has been blind for three days – almost as if dead, or in that tomb with Jesus, symbolically, having undergone his own sort of crucifixion and now resurrection – and Saul gets up and eats and immediately begins proclaiming that Jesus is God's Son.

This is a pretty dramatic transformation. That's the power of Easter. I reflected last week on how the power of Easter turned a bunch of fearful, disheartened disciples into bold evangelists and apostles. In today's story, even more dramatically, an avowed enemy of Jesus is transformed into the person who will become arguably the greatest evangelist the Church has ever known. That doesn't happen because of a mere myth or fairy tale or lie. This sort of transformation happens because of a personal encounter of or with the risen Lord. Even though Saul was not there at the first Easter, even though he didn't witness the resurrection of Jesus personally, he has experienced it for himself in a very personal, direct way. He has been given the opportunity to experience for himself the possibility of new life through the risen Lord. You'd be hard pressed to find a more powerful story of how Easter can change a person's heart and soul and life than this story of Saul/Paul.

The story of Saul, and the story of Peter there in John 21, like the story of Easter, offers us the hope and the possibility of moving beyond our past mistakes – it teaches us the reality of God's forgiveness and love. It teaches us that we all have a part to play, a role to fulfill, in God's plan – if we choose to accept it. It reminds us that God's love is greater than all things, even our past, and even death. And that no one is too far outside, too far removed, too far lost, to be welcomed into God's kingdom. The message of these passages is all about the power of Easter in the lives of Peter and the other disciples and even in the life of villainous Saul, but also hopefully a reminder to each of us of God's offer of new life - a changed life, a transformed life, a life that moves beyond our past and other people's expectations and assumptions about us - and our own expectations and assumptions about ourselves perhaps. Easter offers the reminder of what it means to be made new in the light of God's love. If that offer, if that gift of Easter, was available to Peter, and available to Saul, it certainly is available to us as well.

Amen.

Worried or Weaned?

Luke 10:38-42; Psalm 131

July 21, 2019

Having preached on this story in Luke's Gospel more than once over my 22 years as a pastor, I've discovered that it can be quite controversial, especially for those with a Type A personality. I think you can probably understand why that is – on the surface this story seems to be Jesus rebuking Martha for the work she's doing. Of course the Type A response always is: "But if Martha wasn't doing that work, it wouldn't get done!" which is very true. But I don't think Jesus is rebuking Martha in this story because she is busy. There's much more to it than that.

But first some comments about Mary and Martha. They live in Bethany, which is across the Kidron Valley from the Jerusalem. What's really interesting is that this is the only story about Mary and Martha that occurs in the Synoptic Gospels - Matthew, Mark, and Luke - and this story only appears in Luke. Mary and Martha do not appear in Matthew or Mark. They appear in this story in Luke's Gospel, and then there are a couple other stories about them in John's Gospel. It is John's Gospel that really introduces us to them—it is John who tells us they are the sisters of Lazarus, whom Jesus raises from the dead. John also tells the story of Jesus on his way to Jerusalem for the last time, stopping at Mary and Martha's house, and it is there that Mary is identified as the woman who pours expensive perfume, on Jesus's feet and dries them with her hair. (I will come back to that story a bit later). So in John's Gospel the implication is that the home of Mary and Martha and Lazarus is a place Jesus stops when he is in Bethany, that they are friends. We don't get any of that in the other gospels, and indeed today's story in Luke's Gospel makes it sound like Jesus just happens to stop there, that he hasn't met them before. There is no indication of any relationship beyond this one moment.

So Jesus stops at Mary and Martha's house, and it is Martha who welcomes him. In the context of that day and age this doesn't just mean she said "hello" as he walked through the door, it means she probably offered some water so he could wash up a bit, and some food and refreshments of some kind, and that's probably why we're told she is "busy" – she's getting food ready or if they've already eaten, she is clearing off the table and in the kitchen washing the dirty dishes. Or maybe she realized when Jesus came in that the dog bowl was out in the middle of the living room and there were magazines scattered across the coffee table, and she's clearing things up to make the house more presentable. She is making the house welcoming for their visitor, Jesus.

And as Jesus is sitting there in Mary and Martha's now cleaned up living room after enjoying Martha's hospitality, Mary is just sitting there with him, at his feet, listening. I picture Martha washing dishes and putting away leftovers in the kitchen and Jesus and Mary sitting there in the living room, and I imagine Martha rushing back and forth in front of the open door of the kitchen grumbling a bit, and I imagine you can hear her voice as she goes back and forth, and it fades in and out as she passes by the open door: "grumble grumble grumble...why isn't SHE HELPING me...grumble grumble...and I CAN'T BELIEVE I'M DOING THIS all by myself...grumble grumble" and I imagine maybe some pots and pans being banged together a bit for effect by Martha, you know, just to make sure her sister knows how hard Martha is working while Mary just sits there, and finally Martha comes storming out of the kitchen, maybe waving a ladle or a dishtowel: "JESUS! Doesn't it matter to you that I'm doing ALL the work, and she's just SITTING THERE, doing NOTHING?" I'm sure none of you, especially women, have ever had a situation in which you felt like you were doing all the work at home, right?

So notice what Jesus says—and this is really the crux of the story, Jesus's response to Martha. He says: "Martha, Martha" - notice he has to say her name more than once, he has to get her attention, she is so angry - "Martha, hey Martha, Martha…you are worried and distracted by so many things. There is need of only one thing." Let me point out that Jesus is NOT rebuking her for being busy or doing work. In fact, I'm not sure Jesus is rebuking her at all, that's not the way I hear what he says to her. He's reminding her of something, not rebuking her. He's telling her: "You're worried and distracted," and you don't have to be busy to be worried and distracted. And Jesus goes on: "you're worried and distracted by many things, but there's need of only one thing." So what's really going on here?

I think first Jesus is offering her, reminding her of, a different perspective—suggesting that she would be happier with a different perspective on the situation. Martha is doing good things, necessary things – she's welcoming Jesus to her house and preparing food and showing hospitality, and those are all important. But what Jesus is trying to get her to see is this: "Martha, I am not always going to be here, sitting in your living room." There will always be dishes to wash, or food to prepare, or whatever it is she's doing. But Jesus won't always be sitting in her living room.

This is interesting because it reminds me of that story in John's Gospel that I already mentioned: John's account of Jesus stopping at Mary and Martha's house on his way to Jerusalem. In that story Martha is the one who welcomes him, and Mary is the one who pours this expensive perfume out and dries his feet with her hair. And according to John, at this point Judas Iscariot says: "What a waste. All that expensive perfume could be sold, and the money given to the poor," even though John tells us Judas didn't really care about the poor. Jesus responds to Judas: "You will always have the poor with you, but you won't always have me with you." Jesus isn't saying we shouldn't help the poor but reminding us that there will always be less fortunate people that need our help, but we won't always have Jesus with us to enjoy. You'll always have dirty dishes to wash, and food to prepare, but you won't always have your Lord and Savior sitting in your living room. Jesus is offering a sense of perspective: what's important to be paying attention to right now and what can wait. If Jesus is in your living room, the dirty dishes in the sink can probably wait. Or doing your taxes, or organizing your closet, or mowing the lawn, or checking your email…all those things can wait. If Jesus is sitting in your living room – go sit with Jesus.

So we also get a message about attentiveness as well, about being present and content in the moment. Mary is there hanging on Jesus's every word. Mary somehow seems to know that Jesus, at least as a human being, is not going to be around forever. She somehow knows what's coming for Jesus. So she is taking advantage of this precious, fleeting time to be with him. And this is where I want to bring in Psalm 131, this beautiful, simple little Psalm about quieting our souls – it's really about being with God, although it uses imagery of a mother and a child. "I have calmed and quieted myself, I am like a weaned child with its mother; like a weaned child I am content," I am content to just be with God.

Now I have to admit, because I am a male, and a single male at that, my experience with breastfeeding is limited, to say the least. So this word "weaned" in the Psalm, for many years I just totally missed the meaning of it. I just assumed this Psalm was about a child nursing in its mother's arms. Then finally one day – and I won't reveal how recently this was – I decided to look up the word "weaned." I'm aware that some, maybe all of you, already know what the word actually means, but it was a bit of a revelation to me. To be weaned means to STOP nursing, to literally be withdrawn from your mother's arms. All mammals go through the weaning process at some point as they grow and mature. So the Psalm offers the image of a child who has been weaned, who is no longer nursing but as portrayed in the Psalm, back, for the moment, in Mom's arms.

When a child is nursing, that child probably begins to realize that Mom is going to be picking them up many, many times throughout the day, and the night. Whenever you are hungry, Mom will gather you into her arms to feed you. Once you are weaned, though, those intimate moments in Mom's arms become less common, or at least less necessary for physical survival, not a guaranteed event anymore. So I suspect a weaned child held once again in their mother's arms, realizes: "Hey, I'm not going to waste this time grumbling and fussing and crying, I'm going to simply enjoy this precious time back in Mom's arms, being held by her. I'm going to enjoy it while it lasts because it doesn't happen as often as it did before I was weaned." OK, so maybe I'm giving babies too much credit here, but humor me.

Do you see how that attitude of a weaned child in its mother's arms might apply to Mary here in this story? Mary realizes this time with Jesus, with Jesus right there in the same room with her, sitting in her house, is precious and valuable and will not last forever. It may not occur ever again, in fact. So she is taking advantage of it, enjoying it, drinking it this intimate time with Jesus, and not worrying about dishes or cleaning or anything else. Martha's problem, and our problem far too often, is that she's missing out on this rare and wonderful opportunity of having Jesus right there with her.

I hope you have had moments in your life when you have felt God very close, in your living room, so to speak. But if you are like me, such moments are fleeting, and much too rare. We can't, at least I can't, make them happen – they just happen. Often unexpectedly, like someone dropping by your house unannounced. Now, we can put ourselves in places and moments that make them more likely – in prayer, in worship, perhaps out hiking or doing yard work, out in God's creation, or in family gatherings – but such moments, at least for me, are not a guaranteed and regular occurrence. It's like I've been weaned off them, so when they come now, I need to grab hold of them and appreciate them and enjoy them. So when these moments of closeness with God come, we shouldn't pull out our phones and start checking our messages, or work on our taxes, or start washing dishes – although there are ways to do things like washing dishes in a focused, meditative way – the point is we shouldn't get distracted from such moments by things that will still be there when this precious moment passes. God is always close by, but we don't always feel that, so when we do, we should grab hold and enjoy it. We should all learn to be more like Mary and like that weaned child in the Psalm: "I'm here with Mom. I'm here with God. I'm here with Jesus."

Quiet…

Attentive…

Joyful…

Content…

At Peace…

Because we know these moments don't last.

At least not in this life…

Amen.

Bread, Eggs, Snakes, Scorpions, and Prayer
Luke 11:1-13; Colossians 2:6-19

July 28, 2019

What we find in this passage in Luke's gospel are three little snippets of Jesus discussing prayer. The first section is Luke's account of Jesus giving the model for authentic prayer that we now call "The Lord's Prayer." I'm going to skip over that today, since I preached a series of sermons about the Lord's Prayer a few years ago, and I want to focus today on the second and third snippets of this passage, because that is where things start to get a little strange. There's this odd parable that Jesus tells and then there are these references to snakes and scorpions and eggs and such.

This all begins because the disciples ask Jesus to teach them how to pray. So after giving them a short model for prayer, Jesus offers this parable. He says: "Imagine you go to a friend's house in the middle of the night and you start banging on the door because another friend has shown up at your house and you don't have any bread to give that friend. So you show up at this other friend's house and start banging on the door and yelling: "Hey, get up – I need some bread to give to someone who showed up at my house just now!"" In the context of the culture of Jesus' time, hospitality was a big deal. In this way the Middle East is not dissimilar to the South and its tradition of Southern Hospitality, as many of you know – if someone shows up at your house, you give them refreshments, you give them a whole spread, make them feel at home.

Friendship was also a big deal in this time and culture. If a friend came to you with a request, and you were truly their friend, you would respond, you would honor their request, if at all possible. So in this parable Jesus says: "Imagine that the guy in the house, just woken up from a deep sleep, won't help you, but instead says this: "GO AWAY! It's 3 o'clock in the morning! We're all sleeping, here! I'm not getting up to give you ANYTHING!" In Jesus's time, that response would have been laughable, almost unimaginable, because this so-called friend would have been ashamed to respond that way, not to get up and give you the bread you are asking for. Because that would have shown him to be a fraud, not really a friend at all. That's why Jesus says, as sort of the moral of this parable: "I tell you, even if your friend is a bad friend, and won't get up to help you out of the bonds of friendship, eventually he will get up and give you what you want simply to get rid of you because of your brashness, your persistence, your boldness. Because you keep knocking, knocking, knocking on the door, and eventually just to make you go away and let him get back to sleep, this person will get up and give you the bread you're asking for. He might toss it to you out the window and say a few choice words along with it, but you will get it."

Now this parable is very similar to one that Jesus tells later in Luke's gospel about a persistent widow and an unjust judge. The widow goes to the judge asking for justice, but this judge is a bad judge and won't give it to her. Yet Jesus says: "I tell you because she is persistent, she will eventually get justice, even from this bad judge, by wearing him down." In both parables there is the contrast between a bad friend or a bad judge and our good God. Jesus says: "Think how much more likely God will be to give you what you ask for, to give you bread or justice, than this bad friend or this bad judge, and not because you are persistent but because God is good." And maybe because God never sleeps, too. The point of both parables is that we can be, and should be, bold and persistent in our prayers because God is so much better than a bad friend or a bad judge.

Then Jesus goes on to talk about bad parents. He says: "Even you, you evil human beings, you selfish, sinful people, even you know that when a child asks for a fish, you don't hand them a snake, and if your child gets up in the morning and wants an egg for breakfast, you don't give them a scorpion – that would just be weird." Even we know better than that, and so Jesus says: "If you know how to give good things, imagine how much more God knows this, and is that much more likely to give good things when you ask." And that's why Jesus can tell us: "Ask, and you will receive; seek, and you will find; knock, and the door will be opened." Even at 3 in the morning. Be bold, be persistent, in prayer – because God loves us, and God will answer.

And I was also thinking about what we are to ask for in prayer, because part of what Jesus is saying in this parable is: "Don't be afraid to ask for anything in prayer!" I love our prayer time here in worship at First Presbyterian Church, and the way people are willing to lift up what's on their hearts and minds, but I'll admit there are occasions, every once in a while, when someone will offer a prayer request and I'll think to myself: "That's an odd thing to pray for." But of course who am I to say? So imagine that during prayer time – and I don't think this has ever happened, but just imagine – someone says: "I'm driving to Asheville later today and I pray that I get a good parking spot." Now I have driven in cities, many with worse parking than Asheville, and I've lifted up prayers like that – "God, please let me find a good spot, close to where I'm going. Don't make me drive around for 20 minutes looking for a parking spot." Hey, if that's what you're worrying about in that moment, lift it up to God. That's what prayer is for. All things are open for prayer. Be bold. Be brash.

Let me turn to what Paul writes to the Colossians, because although Paul is not talking about prayer, Paul is reminding us of what we have already been given by God through Christ. He says, for example, in Christ is the fullness of divinity, and that fullness is available to us as well, the fullness of God, the very power of God. In fact one of the things God already has done in Christ is erase "the record" of our sin. Did you hear that in the passage? Any record of our sins has been erased through Christ. Past, present, and future, the record of our sins, our trying to live up to any legal expectations when it comes to God, that has all been erased and "nailed to the cross." Now no one in their right mind would approach God and ask: "Hey, would you erase all my sins by nailing Jesus to the cross?" No one would ever ask for that. No one would be that bold, that brash. But God has already done it, without our asking. God has already given us that, without our asking. And compared to that, nothing else we can possibly ask for in prayer can be foolish or inappropriate. I imagine God saying: "Look, I sent Jesus to earth, to take away all your sins and show you how much I love you – what's a parking space compared to that?" So go ahead and ask for your parking space, or whatever it is that's on your heart, that is causing you anxiety, that is making you worried. Be bold. Be brash. And God will answer.

But be aware that God will not always answer the way you expect. Or in the time frame you might expect or hope. So the fact that you get to Asheville and you have to park a quarter mile away from where you are going does not mean God hasn't heard, and even answered, your prayer. There may be a good reason you didn't find a parking space where you wanted to find one. Maybe there were other people who have more difficulty walking than you do who got those closer parking spaces. Maybe there's a dollar bill on the ground in that spot a quarter mile away that you'll find when you open your car door. I don't know- there may be all sorts of reason you didn't get the parking space you wanted. But it wasn't because God didn't hear or didn't answer your prayer. I'm reminded of – and this will date me a bit – an episode of the TV show M*A*S*H, one of my favorite shows of all time – remember it takes place at a Mobile Army Surgical Hospital in Korea during the Korean war. And in one of the early seasons of the show there's an episode in which a patient shows up to the hospital who claims he is Jesus Christ. And at one point someone, I think it is the Army psychiatrist, Sydney Freedman, is having a conversation with the soldier and he asks: "Does God answer every prayer?" And this soldier who claims to be Jesus replies: "Yes. And sometimes the answer is `no.'" Maybe that's it – God answers every prayer, but sometimes the answer, for our own good, is "no."

But God does answer every prayer, I am certain of that. Again, not always the way we expect or as quickly as we like, but they get answered. So yet more reason to be bold in your prayers. Shameless, even. God doesn't mind. God will not take offense at anything you pray for, not if it is something on your heart and mind at that moment.

I also wanted to note that there is another place in the gospels where Jesus talks about not using a lot of words when we pray. Sometimes we fall into that trap, we think we have to impress God with our prayers: "Ooooh, Great and Loving and Wonderful and Magnificent God, please grant me a safe and convenient spot in which to park mine vehicle after safely enjoying transport through the dangers of the road to the great city of Asheville," you know, we like to make our prayers flowery and formal, as if we're Dorothy talking to the Wizard of Oz, but I'm reminded of something the writer Anne Lamott once said. She said she has two basic prayers: "Thank you, thank you, thank you" and "Help me, help me, help me." That's really all you need when it comes to prayer.

So today we are given some wisdom from Jesus about prayer. And having heard this wisdom, I invite you this week to ask and to seek and to knock and to pray, boldly, and to then to leave the rest in the hands of our good God.

Amen.

Too Much Stuff

Luke 12:13-21; Colossians 3:1-11

August 4, 2019

How many of you have ever looked around your house, opened a closet, gone up into your attic or down into your basement, and thought to yourself: "Boy, I have way too much stuff."

You don't have to raise your hands – I suspect most all of us are in that same boat.

One of my favorite preachers, the late George Carlin – you may know him better as a comedian, but I think he was a great preacher as well, although he might have argued with me on that point – has a famous routine about stuff, about trying to find a place for our stuff. Carlin says that's really the meaning of life, trying to find a place for your stuff. He says that's why we have houses - we have houses because we need a place to put our stuff. You know if we didn't have all that stuff, we wouldn't need houses, and we could just be walking around. A house is really just stuff with a cover over it. And then, when you leave your house, what do you do? You lock the door so no one can get in and take your stuff...while you're out getting more stuff. And sometimes we move to new houses, bigger houses, because we run out of space in the old one for all our stuff.

That's a pretty good segue into the parable that Jesus tells in today's reading from Luke. It's about a guy who discovers he has too much stuff, so he needs to build bigger barns in which to store it. And I suspect that because this parable hits so close to home for many of us, it is not a real favorite of many peoples. Jesus tells this story of a man, a rich man, who reaps an incredible harvest one year, and he ends up with all this extra stuff. And so he says to himself: "What am I going to do? I know, I'll tear down my old barns and build bigger ones to store all my stuff. Then I can just sit back and take it easy." And that very night God comes to this man and says: "You fool. Tonight your life is being taken. And now what's going to happen to all your stuff?"

This is a parable about greed. At least that's how Jesus introduces it. I hope you also noticed that greed is mentioned by Paul in our passage from his letter to the Colossians, as one of the things we should avoid as people who are putting on the "new self" in God. Avoid greed, Paul says, because it is idolatry. One of the problems with all this stuff we have is that our stuff can become idols - replacement gods - in our lives. We can begin to focus our energy and our attention and our time on our stuff. We can begin even to worship our stuff, instead of worshipping God. Our stuff can pull us away from the things of God. As Paul writes, we should "seek the things that are above, set our minds on the things that are above, not on earthly things," not on earthly stuff. And yet we can get so wrapped up in our stuff, that our stuff almost begins to consume us. And, as George Carlin suggests, we then begin to worry excessively about our stuff. We don't just lock our houses so no one can steal our stuff, we buy security systems to protect our stuff, and we buy insurance policies to protect our stuff. And what is it that keeps us up late at night, worrying, fretting, not sleeping? Our stuff. Our stuff becomes our god.

But there's another downside to all our stuff that is revealed in this parable as well, and it is related to greed and idolatry. That's the distraction of stuff: we devote all this time and energy and attention to our stuff and protecting our stuff and this distracts us from what is truly important in life, it distracts us from God and the things of God. You may remember two Sundays ago we read, and I preached about the story of Mary and Martha. Jesus comes to their house and Martha is doing all this work while Mary just sits at Jesus's feet and enjoys being with him and eventually Martha complains about this and Jesus says to her: "Martha, you are worried and distracted by many things." Well, one of the things that can distract us is our stuff. Our stuff can make us worried and distracted and pull us away from God and things that are truly important and of lasting value, those "things that are above." I suppose this aspect has been on my mind recently given the situation with my parents, as I've shared in prayer time. Now my parents are both in pretty good health, but they are both in their mid-80s, and starting to make some decisions about downsizing, about moving out of their house full of stuff and into some sort of independent living facility. So what's going to happen to all their stuff? My mother, especially, has a lot of beautiful family heirlooms that have been passed down through many generations, dishes and stemware and glassware, the stuff we'd bring out once a year for Thanksgiving dinner. I remember when I was younger thinking about how cool it would be someday to have some of that stuff, fancy dishes and glasses, but now—well my Mom was talking the other day about all this stuff and about how we kids would have to divvy it up someday, and I realized I don't have much interest in a lot of the stuff. What do I need sets of fancy dishes for? I haven't thrown a dinner party in.......ever. So, if I ever inherit the dishware, you're all invited to my house for a big fancy dinner party.

My parents are aging. My Mom is about to turn 86 and my Dad will soon be 88. And I'm at that point where I realize that I don't really care about any of their stuff. It seems much more important to just enjoy some time with them; in the remaining time we've got together. That seems so much more important – not the stuff, but the people, the relationships. That realization comes with time, I suppose, with wisdom over the years. Or thinking of a friend that I just heard passed away; he and his wife live nearby, and I hadn't seen him in years. And now I think "Gee, why didn't I take the time to go see him?" That's what's truly important, but we get distracted by stuff and worries about stuff.

One last element about stuff that I find in this parable. This parable is about a man who has an incredible harvest, and builds larger storage bins to put it in. That's not the problem. The big harvest is not the problem. Even building bigger storage bins is not really the problem. I'm always reminded of the story of Joseph when I read this parable. Not Joseph the father of Jesus, but Joseph, the son of Jacob, in Genesis. You remember in the whole soap opera story of Joseph, he ends up in Pharaoh's court, and Pharaoh has this dream of seven fats cows and seven lean cows, and no one can make sense of it until Joseph comes in and says: "this means we are going to have seven good years of harvest and then seven years of famine." So during the seven good years, with Joseph's lead, they store up all the extra grain, so they've got it for the lean years. That's pretty much what the man in the parable does, but there is a crucial difference in the story of Joseph. It is the difference of motivation.

Joseph and the Egyptians, after they have stored up their grain, get word out that they have this grain and they offer it to others, they give it out to people who need it during the lean years. That's what gets Joseph's family to Egypt: they come to access this stored up grain. The motivation is communal. The real problem with the rich man in today's parable is his selfishness. It's not that he had a great harvest or even that he was storing it – it's how he planned to use those riches, that harvest – it's that he was saving it just for his own use and enjoyment. He might have instead said to himself: "Hey, maybe some of my neighbors didn't have such good harvests like I did, and maybe I can share some of my bounty and my harvest with them, in their lean years. Maybe I can take some of my harvest over to the local food bank and let it be shared with those who need it more than I do. Maybe I can share it with others, do some good." But instead in the parable this man says: "I'm just going to keep it all for myself and live it up," and then God comes to him and says: "Bad decision; now the government is going to get all your stuff." This really is a parable about selfishness.

The problem with all of our stuff is that it can make us greedy, distracted, and selfish. That's why it's easier for a camel to go through the eye of a needle than for a rich person to enter the kingdom of God. It's not that God has anything against rich people. It is that our earthly riches can keep us from God, get between us and God, distract us from God, make us selfish. God loves poor people and rich people alike. God just wishes more of us were richer in God rather than richer in stuff.

Amen.

Let's Settle This

Isaiah 1:1, 10-20

August 11, 3019

Today's sermon is political.

I mean according to the dictionary definition of political: *"Of, relating to, or dealing with the affairs of government, the state, or a nation."*

I don't think there's any other honest way to approach today's Scripture reading from Isaiah. In fact many, if not all, of the prophets were political. That's why the book of Isaiah begins the way it does. It tells us who Isaiah is, "Amoz's son" and then it tells us the context in which Isaiah was prophesying. And it doesn't just gives us years, "Isaiah was prophesying between these dates," it tells us who the leaders were, who the kings were - Uzziah, Jotham, Ahaz, and Hezekiah – some of them good kings and at least one of them, Ahaz, awful. Why else would the book of Isaiah begin this way, if not for the fact that these leaders were the people Isaiah was prophesying to or about. Notice as well this first chapter goes on to address "you leaders of Sodom...you people of Gomorrah." Isaiah's prophecies were for leaders and the people of his nation. It's political – focused on what is being done and how things are going in a particular kingdom and in the world.

So what is the message to the people of Isaiah's day, and to us? God says: "I'm fed up. Repulsed, even. I'm fed up with you people. I'm fed up with you and your leaders and your deeds and your worship. You bring your offerings and they are worthless to me because you only listen to me and try to obey me during that time you come to worship, and the rest of the time," as Isaiah will say later in this book, "your hearts are far from me." Or, as Jesus will say to the Pharisees many centuries later: "You worry about cleaning the outside of the cup, but the inside of your cup is filthy." "You go through the motions," God says through Isaiah," your worship does not impact your heart or your actions or your lives the rest of the week."

Ouch.

"I'm fed up," God says, "Fed up because you're not focusing on what I, God, want you to focus on: Justice. What I want you to be paying attention to is helping the oppressed, and defending the orphan, and pleading for the widow."

That refrain – help the oppressed, and the orphan and the widow - runs throughout Scripture, usually with an added fourth element of welcoming the foreigner. To reaffirm that, I looked up some other passages of Scripture that sound very much like this first chapter of Isaiah. This is Exodus 22:21-24: *"Do not mistreat or oppress a foreigner, for you were foreigners in Egypt. Do not take advantage of the widow or the orphan. If you do and they cry out to me, I will certainly hear their cry. My anger will be aroused, and I will kill you with the sword; your wives will become widows and your children orphans."*

Deuteronomy 27:19: *"Cursed is anyone who withholds justice from the foreigner, the orphan or the widow. Then all the people shall say, "Amen!"*

From the prophet, Zechariah, chapter 7, verse 9-10: *"This is what the Lord Almighty said: 'Administer true justice; show mercy and compassion to one another. Do not oppress the widow or the orphan, the foreigner or the poor.'"*

And another prophet, here is Malachi chapter 3, verse 5: *"So I will come to put you on trial. I will be quick to testify...against those who defraud laborers of their wages, who oppress the widows and the orphans, and deprive the foreigners among you of justice, but do not fear me," says the Lord Almighty."*

Ouch. Are you sensing the pattern here?

And just in case you think these are only Old Testament sentiments, I came across this in the first chapter of James in my morning devotions yesterday: *"Religion that God our Father accepts as pure and faultless is this: to look after orphans and widows in their distress and to keep oneself from being polluted by the world."* (James 1:27)

"Help the oppressed – the widows, the orphans, the poor, the strangers, the foreigners – that's what I want you to do," God says. "And I'm fed up if you're coming to worship and that isn't any part of your worship."

One of the commentators I was reading this week, Paul Simpson Duke, put it bluntly: "Worship unconcerned with justice is obscene."

Ouch.

Focus on justice. Help the oppressed, the poor, the widow, the orphan. How are we doing at that? Justice always involves the larger group, the community, the country, the nation. So I was doing some thinking and pondering about all of this and about some of the specific issues that have been in the news recently, that we are trying to deal with as people, as a nation, as a world. And pondering what this passage might tell us as Christians about how we should approach these issues.

Thank God there haven't been any more mass shootings since last weekend when there were 2 within the space of 13 hours in El Paso and Dayton. When it comes to the issue of mass shootings and guns, who are the oppressed? Are the gun manufacturers the oppressed? Is the National Rifle Association the oppressed? (I'm old enough to remember when the NRA used to be focused on promoting gun safety, rather than lobbying on behalf of the gun manufacturers.) Are gun owners the oppressed? From a Christian perspective, does God really want individuals to have access to weapons that can shoot a hundred bullets in one minute? Is that something God desires, honestly? I'm not sure God cares about the 2nd Amendment, I'm not sure God cares about our entire Constitution or any constitution, except and only as far as they promote justice and help the oppressed. Does God want God's children to have weapons that can kill so many people so quickly? Does God want us to have nuclear weapons? Well, that's for another sermon. Back to the question – who are the oppressed when it comes to mass shootings and guns in this country? Are you oppressed if the government says: "For the safety of everyone and the good of society, we're not going to allow any private citizen to own a weapon and a magazine for it that allow you to shoot that many bullets that quickly." Is that oppression? Or are the oppressed here those innocent victims and their families, those who are now widows and orphans because someone else had a weapon that could shoot that many bullets? Who are the oppressed? And how might we help them?

In our current immigration crisis, who are the oppressed? Are we, this great nation, this rich nation, that people are desperately trying to come to for a better life, for greater opportunity, are we the oppressed? Is it the families separated at the border, families whose reasons for being at the border you may disagree with, but the fact is they are often separated, and some of the children end up living in conditions that, if you found out your child was living in similar conditions while at summer camp, you'd immediately be on the phone complaining – who are the oppressed in this immigration crisis? And how can we help them?

Who is oppressed when it comes to poverty and economic inequality in this country? Are we the citizens oppressed if our government uses some of our taxes to fund programs to help those who are living in poverty? Is that oppression? Who is oppressed when the top 1% have so much wealth and so many at the bottom of that financial spectrum have almost nothing, and many don't have homes in which to live or know where their next meal will come from?

In terms of the healthcare debate in this country, who are the oppressed? The insurance companies, are they the oppressed? The pharmaceutical companies, the private hospital chains, are they the oppressed? Or is it the person forced to make a decision between spending money for healthcare and medication or buying food, or paying rent – in this, the richest country in the world? Who are the oppressed? And how can we help them?

Are white people oppressed in this country? Even when some other ethnic groups who have always been a part of this country are demanding that we white people give up the tiniest, miniscule amount of the power and privilege we have enjoyed since day one in this country, does that mean we are suddenly oppressed? Are we Christians oppressed in this country? There are Christians being oppressed in other parts of the world, but just because someone wishes us "Happy Holidays" rather than "Merry Christmas," does that mean we are oppressed?

I think this passage in Isaiah screams at us, as Christians, to look at all these situations, and more, in our country, in our world, and always ask the questions: "Who are the oppressed here? And how can we help them?"

In terms of how we might help, the possibilities are wide and diverse. I know, for example, some people who have their Representatives and Senator's office phone numbers on speed dial, so they often call to make their opinions known. Others write letters, send emails, to those in positions of leadership and authority. Others march and protest in places like Raleigh and Washington D.C. and visit their representatives in person to express their views. Others look for ways to help closer to home, ways they can get involved in their own communities to help the oppressed. Friends, there are all sorts of such opportunities, even here in our little corner of the world, to get involved, to do something, to help those less fortunate and much more oppressed than us.

Maybe just being more aware of how you and I treat every single person we meet every day. I mentioned at the beginning of the service the woman who stopped me earlier this morning at the grocery store to compliment my tie – such a small little thing, it took her all of 3 seconds to smile and tell me she liked my tie, but it made my day. I don't often get compliments on how I dress. Now that is not directly confronting oppression, but there are a lot of people we encounter in the world who are doing just the opposite of what this woman took 3 seconds to do – I see a lot of people who don't look very happy and they want other people to know it, and when they scowl at me, I start to get a little, well, depressed, if not oppressed. When you are in the checkout line at the store and there are 3 people ahead of you and the line is moving so slowly because the cashier is doing an awful job, they must be a trainee or something, and you've got places to go and things to do, and by the time you get up there and you've had a bad day, too – but are you going to take it out on that cashier? Pass along the oppression to that person who is making maybe $7.25 an hour, or will you make the effort to smile and say: "Thank you. It looks like you're having a bad day, I hope it gets better." A small little gesture, but you might make that person's day a little less oppressive. You might be the only person who smiles at them that day. In fact, this week, smile at every single person you meet or pass. Big, broad smile to everyone. Sure, half the people will probably think you're nuts, but your smile might be the only one they see the entire day.

Finally, something else we can all do is pray. Even as we find ways to help lift up those who are oppressed, be lifting them up in your prayers as well. And lift up the oppressors, too. Pray for the leaders of our country and our world, even if you think they are doing a horrible job. Pray that they might find wisdom and compassion, a change of heart, a different perspective, to do a better job. It can't hurt.

"I'm fed up," God says, "in fact I am repulsed by your worship, by your actions, you have blood on your hands because you are not working for justice."

I don't know about you, but when I hear words like that, that God is fed up, especially with our worship – that makes me tremble in my boots and fall to my knees and strive to try to do better. I don't want God fed up with me anymore.

Amen.

Clearly Jesus Was Just Misquoted
Luke 12:49-56

August 18, 2019

"Do you think that I have come to bring peace to the earth? No, I tell you, I have come instead to bring division."

(Sigh)

I really wish Jesus hadn't said that.

You know, maybe Jesus didn't say it. How do we know that this is actually what Jesus said? How do we know Luke didn't just get it wrong, misquote Jesus? Yeah, I think Jesus was misquoted. I don't think Jesus actually said this.

Amen.

Well, that was easy.

Unfortunately, it is too easy to just dismiss or ignore passages in the Bible that we'd rather not have to deal with, that are difficult or challenging. The problem is once you allow yourself to dismiss something like "I have come to bring division," the next thing you know people are dismissing "take up your cross and follow me," or "love your enemies."

So, although we don't know for sure that Jesus actually said all the things attributed to him, at least according to Luke, and, it is worth noting, according to Matthew as well, Jesus did say this. (In Matthew's version, Jesus says "I have not come to bring peace but to bring a sword," which is maybe even more troubling.) According to Luke, Jesus said: "I have come instead to bring division," so we have to figure out why Jesus might have said this, and what message Jesus is trying to tell us.

Let me start with some context which I think begins to answer those questions. This passage occurs in a part of Luke's gospel after the moment when Luke states: "Jesus set his face toward Jerusalem." That's in Luke 9:51. "Jesus set his face toward Jerusalem," which means that everything after that moment is focused on what Jesus is going to do, his purpose for being on earth. He's focused on Jerusalem and what will happen there, he's focused on confronting the religious and political authorities there, and he's focused on the results of his being in Jerusalem – his arrest, his crucifixion, and ultimately his resurrection. So after that moment in Luke's gospel when Jesus sets his face to Jerusalem, Jesus is focused on why he has come and what he is going to do. It is in that context, with that focus, that Jesus says: "I have a baptism I must go through, and how I wish it were already come, I'm distressed until it is completed. Do you think I have come to bring peace? No, I tell you, not peace but division."

The next question, and maybe the big question to ask: when Jesus says that about bringing division, is his statement prescriptive or descriptive? If this statement is prescriptive, Jesus would be saying: "Here is what I am intending to happen, here is what I want to happen." Is Jesus saying he came with the intention, the purpose, of creating division? That would be prescriptive as when a doctor writes a prescription, intending for you to follow it and fill it and use it. Is Jesus speaking prescriptively, telling us the reason for what he is doing? Or is Jesus speaking descriptively, that is describing what will result from what he is doing? Is Jesus saying that division is part of what he has come to do, or is the division simply one of the results, the side-effects, of what he has come to do? Prescriptive or descriptive?

I believe, and I'm going to suggest, that Jesus is speaking descriptively here. This division he predicts is not what Jesus intends or wants, but it will be one of the results of his preaching and teaching and actions. Partly because what Jesus has come to do requires his followers to make choices. And choices almost always create division. So Jesus comes and basically says: "You must choose – if you follow me, if that's the choice you make, that means you're choosing not to put other things as your top priority. Are you going to choose to give the highest authority to earthly rulers or to me? Are you going to give your primary allegiance to a country or a nation or an institution or a Party or a person, or to me?" And that choice is going to create division, as choices always do. When the last time your family tried to make a choice about where to eat dinner? Did it create any argument, any division? Choices create division because different people make different choices. Not everyone in the world was going to choose, or chooses today, to follow Jesus, and that means there's going to be division and tension between people.

But even beyond the choice, there is going to be division in following Jesus because Jesus comes to bring change – to change us and to change our world. Change, transformation, is what Jesus was always talking about. A new creation. "YOU are a new creation, I come to make all things new, including you, which means you must change. I come to change the world." And change always creates division…especially from those who don't want things to change or feel they don't need to change. Jesus comes to turn everything upside down, and it is not just in this passage that Jesus talks about that. Think about those times Jesus says: "The first will be last, and the last will be first." If you are - right now, here in this world – last, that's good news. If you are - right now, here in this world - first, that's not such good news and you might not want to hear it and certainly not to follow it. And thus there is division. Think of the parable that Jesus told about workers in a vineyard – remember that one? In which the workers who were hired first thing in the morning were promised a fair day's wage, and at the end of the day, those who were hired for just the last hour of the day were paid first, and were paid a full day's wage, so the workers hired first thought they'd get more, and when they were given the same full day's wage, they got angry. They thought they deserved more. And they are not happy about the owner's generosity.

Jesus comes to overturn the status quo. So if you like and are happy with the status quo, with things how they are right now, you might be resistant to his message and his purpose. Jesus comes saying, "If you choose to follow me, you must change. But I also come to change the world. If you follow me you must make a choice, and if you follow me you must be open to change." Which means, in this sense at least, you cannot be a conservative Christian. There is no such thing. You can't follow Jesus and hold on to the past, to things as they are, or as they once were. Jesus didn't come to conserve the past. Jesus came to change the future, to change our world, to change us.

You see how this might get divisive? Not everyone is open to change. Not everyone is open to change in their own lives. We get comfortable with things the way they are, even if they aren't perfect. We prefer the devil we know to the devil, or angel, we don't know. Change is risky. Following Jesus is risky. Making choices is risky.

I think Jesus is telling us in this passage that if we make the choice to follow him, if we open ourselves to the changes that choice may bring, this is going to cause division. This isn't God's fault; it isn't Jesus's fault. It's our fault – our fault as imperfect humans who don't want to change or be changed. Especially those of us who enjoy a certain amount of power and privilege in the world as it currently exists. Jesus says: "I come to lift up the lowly and bring down the powerful," and in saying such things he echoes his mother, Mary, who says exactly that in Luke chapter 1, in her great "Magnificat" – she just uses more poetic language and we set it to beautiful music and forget what a radical, earth-shattering, divisive statement she makes there. The prophets preached this, too – this need for choice and change and the resulting division. When God's kingdom comes, not everyone is going to rejoice. But again that is our fault for not wanting to be forced to change, to make a choice. God does not create these divisions; Jesus does not create these divisions. We create them by our reluctance to follow.

"Love your enemies" – that's tough.

"Take up your cross and follow me" – that's tough.

"Work for love and justice, help the oppressed" – that's tough.

If any of this were easy, everyone would be doing it.

So I read these words of Jesus about division as descriptive: "Here, unfortunately, is what is going to happen as a result of what I've come to do. It is not what I want to happen, but because you are imperfect children trying to follow your perfect Savior, there is going to be tension and division."

So now perhaps the most important question – how do we as Christians deal with that division? I don't think we are meant to seek out or exacerbate division, but we are called to make certain choices that, through our making them, cause division. We are called to be open to change that may cause division. But we are called to do these things in the most loving, peaceful way possible. But that may not always be possible. So there's this fine line we are called to walk, on one side the awareness that following Christ truly, authentically, sincerely, brings with it division, and on the other trying to figure out how we minimize or limit that division or maybe even bring other people along, slowly, patiently, so there is less division than there might have been. This is not an easy task, obviously. And we always have to err on the side of following Christ, even if this creates division.

But there is hope. There will not always be this division between human beings. Recall that interesting statement Jesus makes about his work: "How I am distressed until it's completed." Maybe that's where we are as a world right now. Jesus's whole purpose has not been completed - we, and all creation, still groan as we await all things being made new, we are in distress, the distress of division and turmoil, in the meantime. But that's not the way things always will be.

As we continue to work for love and justice and peace, as we continue to make those choices along the way and work for change, we have to be confident that ultimately these things will indeed happen. There's hope. All things will be made new. All will turn out well, all manner of things will be well, ultimately...just not yet. In the meantime we are called to work for love, justice, peace, and goodwill, and to do so as lovingly and peacefully as we can. And to do so knowing that although we aren't there yet, we will get there. We will all get there together. And that's when all division will end.

Amen.

One Bride for Seven Brothers
Luke 20:27-40

November 10, 2019

Jesus would have been a great politician.

I mean that literally. Wouldn't it be great if we had 535 Jesuses in Congress and one in the White House, too?

But by saying that I also mean Jesus answered questions well, as we see in today's story in Luke's Gospel. It begins with a group of religious leaders called the Sadducees coming to Jesus and posing a question.

Before considering their question and the answer Jesus gives, let's first remember who the Sadducees are because that is germane to what they are doing here. In the time Jesus lived, Scripture tells us about at least two sets of prominent religious leaders: the Sadducees and the Pharisees. The Pharisees are probably more familiar to us, since they appear more often in the Gospel accounts, usually cast in the role of the "bad guys," but the Pharisees were, ironically, the more progressive of these two groups of religious leaders. The Sadducees were quite conservative and by that I mean they based their theology and practice solely on the books of Torah, the first five books of the Hebrew Scriptures - Genesis, Exodus, Leviticus, Numbers, and Deuteronomy - and they didn't ascribe divine inspiration to any other books of the Hebrew Bible. Thus everything they preached and practiced they did because they found warrant for it in those first five books of the Bible. That's why they did not believe in resurrection or an afterlife because they did not find any evidence for those things in Torah. In comparison, the Pharisees were actually quite liberal, they found divine inspiration in other Hebrew Scriptures, including fairly recent books like Daniel, which clearly alludes to an afterlife and resurrection. The Pharisees also relied on oral traditions, not just on written Scriptures, for inspiration, which further distanced them from the Sadducees.

So it is the Sadducees who approach Jesus in today's story, and although they do not believe in resurrection, they note that Jesus has been talking about resurrection – predicting his own resurrection, but also talking about God's coming kingdom and at least pointing towards the hope that his followers, too, might be resurrected – and so the Sadducees come and ask Jesus a question.

Now there are many reasons we humans ask questions. Sometimes we ask questions because we actually want to know the answer, to learn something new, like students in a class posing questions to their teacher so they can better understand what they are being taught. But sometimes we ask questions not because we want to know the answer but because we think we already know the answer and we're testing the person, or we think the answer will make them look foolish, will be indefensible, and by trying to answer our question the other person will end up looking bad. These are so-called "gotcha" questions, asked sometimes during Presidential debates or on cable TV talk shows, designed to trip someone up. This is the sort of question the Sadducees ask Jesus, and they ask it for the sole purpose of making him look foolish and stupid for preaching about resurrection, because they don't think there really IS an answer to their question, at least not one that can be logically based on Torah. And it is from Torah, from the law of Moses, from Deuteronomy chapter 25 specifically, that they draw this hypothetical question. In Deuteronomy 25, Moses says that if a man marries a woman and he dies before he has produced an heir, the husband's brother has the duty to then marry his deceased brother's wife and produce an heir and carry on the family name. And if that brother refuses, the widow is actually allowed to publicly spit in his face.

So the Sadducees, armed with this law regarding "levirate marriage" as it is known, pose Jesus a question: "Teacher," they say - and you can almost hear the smug tone in their voices – "Teacher, we have a question. You are so learned that you certainly remember Moses pronouncing this obligation in Deuteronomy. Now suppose there is a man who married a woman, but he died before he had any children with his wife. Now this man had six brothers, and each one in succession followed this law and married this woman, the first brother's wife, and yet each in turn died childless. So Teacher..." and you can see their smirking smug smiles growing as they lean in for the kill, for the question they are so sure will trap Jesus, "Teacher, in the resurrection that you talk about, in this afterlife you seem to believe in, whose wife will this woman be, which of the seven brothers?"

They think they've got Jesus; they think they have trapped him; they think they have posed a question for which there is no possible response, at least no possible response drawn from Torah. But Jesus is way ahead of them, he sees right through what they are attempting to do. So Jesus replies: "Actually, you've got it all wrong. It has nothing to do with marriage or any law in Torah. You're just wrong about God's kingdom and resurrection."

"First of all," Jesus continues," Let's talk about marriage..."

What's the purpose of marriage? What is the reason that human society is so involved with and interested in promoting the institution of marriage? The purpose of marriage, at least from society's perspective, is to bring people together to produce offspring, to have children, sort of like in Deuteronomy chapter 25. Now why does human society want people to have children? To perpetuate itself, to keep society alive. And why do we have to worry about keeping society alive? Because we humans die. So if there aren't any children produced through marriage, society itself will die. The primary purpose of marriage, at least in the eyes of society, is to promote the bearing and raising of children and the perpetuation of society because we human beings as a species and as societies would die off otherwise.

Jesus reminds the Sadducees that he is talking about resurrection and the afterlife, "heaven," if you want to attach that word to it. And what does that mean? It means living eternally, forever, with God. So if in the afterlife people live forever and don't die, there's no reason for marriage in the afterlife. There's no need for procreation because you don't have to worry about perpetuating the human race anymore because no one is going to die. So Jesus continues: "There's no marriage in heaven, there's no need for it. In fact, Sadducees, the problem is that you are thinking about God's kingdom as if it were like an earthly kingdom. You are assuming that in heaven there will be all the rules and regulations and customs and institutions that we have here on earth, many of which have to do with suffering and death. There will be no need for any of those things on heaven, in the afterlife. In fact, in heaven it won't matter what country you lived in, or what race you were, or what family connections you might have had, or how much money you had – none of those things that matter on earth will matter in heaven. In heaven, EVERYONE is simply a child of God. The woman and all seven of the brothers will all be simply children of God, fully and completely, and it won't matter who was married to whom. Your worth in heaven is not based on any relationship to any other human being, but solely on your relationship to God."

What Jesus is saying here is that God's kingdom is about life. It is a kingdom of LIFE – life abundantly, life richly, life eternally. And notice that Jesus brilliantly uses Torah, those five books the Sadducees ascribed to, as the basis of his answer. Jesus says: "I can prove the validity of what I am saying by the very same books of Torah you created your hypothetical question from." In Torah, you remember when Moses encountered God at the burning bush and he asked God, "Who are you?" And God first replied, "I AM," and Moses says, "Well if I am going to go to my fellow Hebrews, just saying "I AM" has sent me might not be enough, it's kind of vague, can you give me a bit more detail about who you are?" And God says: "I AM the God of Abraham and the God of Isaac and the God of Jacob." All of them long dead by the time of Moses. "I AM their God." Notice God doesn't say: "I was the God of Abraham, and of Isaac, and of Jacob." God says, "I AM their God." God speaks in present tense. "I AM their God" because they are obviously still living...with God. God is the God of life, and God's kingdom is one of life – abundant and eternal. "By asking your question, O Sadducees," Jesus concludes, "you clearly don't yet understand that."

Now you might understand why Luke tells us that the Sadducees said to themselves: "Let's not ask Jesus any more questions like that again." Jesus turns a question designed to trap him and make him look foolish into a deep, profound answer about who God is and what God's kingdom is like. God is all about life, and not the petty rules and regulations and assumptions and institutions of this world. We must leave those behind when thinking about the nature of God's kingdom and about God. Our God is a God of life. One of the things we struggle to get our minds around in our earthly life is that all, or most all, of the things we get so wrapped up in and focused on in this life – laws and rules and regulations and customs and institutions and flags and borders – God doesn't really care about...except as they may or may not reflect the values of God's kingdom in some way. God doesn't really care about marriage or traffic laws or taxes or political parties or nations – God ultimately cares about one thing: God wants us - all of us, each of us, every single human being - to live. To live abundantly and eternally with God. That's all that really matters, at least to God. And thus maybe it's all that should matter, ultimately, to us, too.

Amen.

King of the Cross

Colossians 1:15-20; Luke 23:33-43

Christ the King Sunday
November 24, 2019

It can be interesting and enlightening to consider passages of Scripture out of the usual context in which we are used to hearing them. I think that is certainly true for today's reading from Luke, his account of the crucifixion of Jesus. We are used to hearing this story in the context of Holy Week and Good Friday, and in that context what usually stands out in this story, at least to me, is the incredible suffering our Lord endured and the injustice of it all and the fact Jesus went through all this for our sake. Reading the account of the crucifixion on Christ the King Sunday, this Sunday that we set aside for considering the reign of Christ as our true king, a couple different things struck me. One is the fact that Jesus is actually described as "King of the Jews" a couple of times, but always as a way of mocking him – that's why Pontius Pilate has that sign hung on the cross declaring: "This is the King of the Jews," and why the soldiers and the crowds mock Jesus, some of them even saying: "If you are King of the Jews, save yourself." The irony, of course, is that Jesus really is their King, and ours - not just King of the Jews, but the True King of All Creation. The second thing that strikes me in reading this passage on this particular Sunday is all the qualities Jesus demonstrates in the Luke passage, and that are attributed to him in that great hymn of praise in Colossians, that remind us what sort of king he really is and what his kingdom is really all about. These many kingly qualities are what really jumped out at me as I considered these passages in the context of Christ the King Sunday.

So what are some of these qualities of being a king – a truly good king and ruler – that jump out of these readings? Well, you may have noticed some yourself, but let me offer you my list of qualities that I noticed in these passages.

I think the first kingly quality that jumps out at me is compassion and love. Jesus is a king who has compassion for people, who demonstrates love in everything he says and does, even here at the moment of his crucifixion and death. It has been said that people reveal who they really are when they are at a low point, and here in this moment of suffering and death, Jesus demonstrates, as he always did, what a loving, compassionate king he is. This is shown most clearly in his demonstration of forgiveness, another quality of his kingdom and his kingly nature. It is amazing to me that here Jesus is on the cross, being crucified, suffocating to death in one of the most horrible ways imaginable, and he deliberately and publicly forgives the very people who are putting him to death and mocking him while doing so. Jesus is a compassionate king who is all about forgiveness, and that forgiveness is unconditional, since he offers it to those who are in the very process of killing him, who are responsible for him being on that cross, including us. They haven't done anything to earn forgiveness, but he forgives them nonetheless: "Father, forgive them, for they don't know what they are doing." Jesus is a king who loves and forgive - very much unlike most earthly kings and rulers.

Also unlike most earthly kings and rulers, Jesus demonstrates humility. He is a humble king. So ironic, because if any king or ruler ever had reason to be narcissistic and self-absorbed and arrogant, it is the King of all Creation. But the very fact that Jesus is on that cross at all shows how humble he is. As the apostle Paul told the Philippians, Jesus is all about emptying himself and humbling himself, even to the point of death, even death on a cross - such a public, humiliating, excruciating way to die. Jesus is a king who is focused on serving and giving of himself, not trumpeting and lifting up himself.

This leads to another quality exhibited by our King here in this passage, and that is the fact that he saves others, not himself. Everyone keeps saying to Jesus: "Save yourself. If you really were the Messiah, the Christ, the King of the Jews, you would save yourself." And what Jesus actually demonstrates is how woefully they misunderstand what it means to be King. What Jesus demonstrates is that he is truly our King, the King of all people, because Jesus gives himself for us and for all people. The last thing a true king, a real leader and ruler, would do is save themselves while others perish. So Jesus humbles himself and allows himself to die in order to save everyone else, including us.

Another kingly quality that Jesus demonstrates is peacemaker. The writer of Colossians declares that Jesus "brought peace through the blood of the cross." Jesus is a king who is all about promoting peace, in all aspects – not just peace in our world, among nations and peoples, but peace even in our own hearts. Unlike so many earthly kings and rulers, Jesus does not promote violence or war or conquest. Jesus is not a king who divides people, but who unites them, who brings them together, who brings peace within families, communities, nations, and all creation. We all are unified by Jesus in that moment of his crucifixion – he is doing it for all of us, for all creation. Jesus is not just a king who promotes peace, he is also a king who works for reconciliation. The whole point of the Incarnation and the crucifixion was to reconcile us with God and with each other. Jesus is a king who unites people, who brings them together, who builds bridges, not walls. As awful as this moment of Jesus on the cross is, it is in this very moment that Jesus shows that he is truly a king who reconciles people, who brings peace, who unites people and God and all creation.

And speaking of all creation, another quality Jesus demonstrates as our heavenly king is especially pronounced in that great hymn in our Colossians reading: Jesus is a king who creates. The writer of Colossians declares that Jesus, as the Son, is "first over all creation," and that "all things were created by him...through him, and for him." Jesus was there at the moment of creation, and Jesus is a king who creates, who builds up, who lifts up, who literally holds all things together. Jesus is a not a king or a ruler who tears things and people down, who sows chaos and division and destruction in his wake as so many earthly kings and rulers do and have done. Jesus builds up and creates, he brings life - that is the nature of his kingdom. Related to this is the statement in Colossians that declares "all the fullness of God was pleased to live" in Jesus, as king. Jesus is full of God, full of love, full of divinity, as opposed to other things that some of our earthly rulers and kings are full of.

The last kingly quality I want to mention is demonstrated by that profound and moving interaction Jesus has with the second of the two criminals being crucified with him. Jesus is being crucified between two criminals, whose crimes remain nameless, and one of them joins in the mocking of Jesus along with most everyone else there that day, which is pretty amazing in and of itself – I mean, he is wasting his remaining breath to mock the person on the cross next to him. But the other criminal, with his last breath, rebukes the first criminal, reminds him that they both deserved the punishment they are receiving for whatever they have done, he is confessing that his crucifixion is just and deserved but somehow he knows that Jesus, unlike them, is innocent. And he then utters that plaintive cry at the end of our story and the end of his remaining breath: "Jesus, remember me when you come into your kingdom." Now I don't think Jesus and this criminal have ever met before, they are strangers to each other, but clearly this criminal has either heard about Jesus or just knows, intuitively, who Jesus is, what Jesus is like. So he asks, "Remember me, when you come into your kingdom," and he even calls Jesus by his name, which not many people ever do in the gospels. "Remember me, WHEN you come into YOUR kingdom." This criminal clearly believes that Jesus is indeed a king, indeed his king. It is a poignant and profound request he makes here in his dying moments.

And Jesus replies: "Yes. I assure you that today you will be with me in paradise, in my kingdom." Jesus is a king who remembers people, who remembers and acknowledges every single person in his kingdom, every single one of us. I'll bet Jesus is great at remembering people's names. No one is too small, too insignificant, too far away, too cut off, for Jesus to notice and remember and reach out to, even as he is dying on the cross. Unlike so many earthly kings and rulers who forget about people, who play favorites, who dismiss whole groups and populations in their own kingdoms, Jesus is a king who remember and respects each and every person in his kingdom. And who invites each and every person to be part of the kingdom.

I think there are a number of things we are to take away and to carry with us from this Sunday when we acknowledge and consider Jesus as our true heavenly King. One is for us as, hopefully, part of his kingdom, to more and more act like our king, to follow his example, to strive to follow his model, to embody as best we can the qualities we've talked about today - compassion, humility, forgiveness, reconciliation, peacemaking, building up, remembering others. But also there is the perhaps even simpler and more profound reminder today that Jesus remembers you and acknowledges you as part of his kingdom. And to know and hold onto that promise he makes to all of us that today we might be with him as part of his kingdom. And for us to keep doing what we can to ensure that we continue to be part of that kingdom, each and every day.

Amen.

Like a Thief?
Matthew 24:36-44

First Sunday of Advent
December 1, 2019

And so we begin Advent with these traditional, heartwarming images: a devastating flood; a kidnapping; and a thief breaking into your house.

I don't know about you, but I find this passage in Matthew a little unsettling, to say the least. Jesus is talking about when he, the Son of Man, will come again. That is, of course, part of this season of Advent. We often think of this season as being about preparing for Christmas, and I know as a kid that's how I always thought of Advent – the four-week countdown to when Santa came and I got presents. Oh, and the birth of Jesus. Part of the season of Advent involves preparing for an event that has already happened, in the past, about 2000 years ago. But this season also reminds us that we live our entire lives in a sort of Advent - waiting for what is "not yet," for what is yet to come, the coming of Christ a second time. That's what Jesus is talking about here in Matthew 24, about that time when he will come again. But I have to wonder why he uses these disturbing and unsettling images to describe what his coming again will be like.

The first image or analogy Jesus offers is the flood that occurred in the time of Noah – you know, that flood that wiped out everyone in the entire world, every single creature except for Noah and his immediate family and those pairs of animals he gathered into the ark. So the analogy is to a horrible, devastating flood that no one except Noah knew was coming. Strange that Noah doesn't appear on too many Hallmark cards this time of year. It's a troubling image – an unexpected, devastating flood. According to Jesus that is what the coming of the Son of Man will be like.

Maybe even more troubling is the next image Jesus offers to describe his second coming: it will be like two men working the field and one of them is simply taken away and vanishes while the other remains, like two women working at a mill and without warning one of them vanishes and the other remains. Jesus doesn't even let us in on which of the people is the lucky one – the one who vanishes or the one who remains? The only thing that seems clear is that the Son of Man will come back like an invisible kidnapper.

Then we get to the third image, and this is the one I find most troubling and the one I want to take some time to consider in detail: when the Son of Man comes again, he will come like a thief in the night, and if the homeowner had only known exactly when the thief was coming, he could have prevented him from breaking in.

Now I get what Jesus is trying to tell us here, with all these analogies. The coming of the Son of Man will be unexpected and we need to stay alert for it. But why compare it to a thief coming in the night? Other books of the Bible use this same language - 1 Thessalonians compares the coming of the Son of Man to a thief in the night, as does 2 Peter and multiple passages in the Book of Revelation. But if all Jesus was really trying to tell us was that his coming again will be unexpected, why couldn't he have used a happier analogy? "The coming of the Son of Man will be like opening your front door on Thanksgiving and seeing that long lost cousin you haven't seen for twenty years standing there." Or "The coming of the Son of Man will be like a surprise birthday party." Why a thief?

By using the analogy of a thief in the night, Jesus is clearly telling us, among other things, that the coming of the Son of

Man will be unexpected, and not just unexpected, but unknown. Did you notice at the beginning of today's passage that interesting comment that Jesus makes? He says: "Only the Father knows the day and the time when the Son of Man will return. The angels don't know, I don't even know." I will leave you to ponder the Trinitarian complications that arise from his comment; I'll just mention the irony that ever since Jesus said this, human beings have been bending over backwards trying to figure out the exact time when he would return. Throughout history many have thought they figured it out, and were able to pinpoint an exact day even, and, so far, all of them have been wrong. More ironic is that they all have missed seeing their own arrogance in attempting to figure out something that Jesus himself says he doesn't know. The coming of the Son of Man will not just be unexpected, it is unknown, even to the Son himself. So it is like the arrival of a thief – if you knew when the thief was coming, well, that would solve the problem, wouldn't it? But the whole point, at least from the thief's perspective, is that they don't want you to know when they are coming.

The coming of a thief is also unseen. This is why most thieves, at least the successful ones, don't rob houses in the middle of the day. They do it at night when it is dark, and they won't be seen. So Jesus seems to be telling us that the coming of the Son of Man will be unseen and perhaps will even occur in a manner that we can't begin to imagine. I mean, how do you know by what means a thief will break into your house? It could be through the door, through a window, through the chimney, maybe through the internet – thieves today don't even need to physically enter your house to steal from you. Does this mean that Jesus will come again in a way we don't have a clue about, in a way we can't even envision – invisible and unseen?

Another oddity about Jesus describing his coming as being like a thief in the night is that we try to protect ourselves from thieves and do our best to prevent them from succeeding. We buy home security systems and alarms and safes and locks and big dogs. I'm wondering what the spiritual equivalent of a home security system is. What's the spiritual equivalent of door locks and fireproof safes and barking dogs? Faith? Trust? The recognition that we aren't as prepared as we should be? When it comes to thieves, we do our best to prevent them from coming, too, not just protecting ourselves. By using this analogy of a thief, is Jesus telling us that his coming back is something we might want to prevent? Maybe to give ourselves more time to get ready? I'm reminded of Simon Peter writing that maybe God is delaying the end of the world because God wants more and more people to be ready and avoid perishing. If Jesus comes like a thief in the night, does that mean we should be trying to prevent Jesus from coming?

And if Jesus comes like a thief, does that mean that the coming of Jesus is illegal, outside of the law? After all, that's what makes a thief a thief – they operate outside the law. If the thief just knocked on your front door and politely asked you to give them your stereo, they wouldn't be a thief. Is Jesus trying to tell us that he comes outside the law, maybe beyond the law? And if so, what law? Traffic laws? Tort law? Tax law? God's law? The laws of physics? Jesus is the one who said he came not to abolish the law but to fulfill it. But a thief doesn't "fulfill" the law, the thief breaks it. How does that apply to the second coming of Jesus?

Have you noticed I am leaving you with a lot of unanswered questions? Well, just a few more.

A thief comes to steal. That's the purpose of a thief – to steal something from someone else. When Jesus comes again, will he steal something from us? Certainly not our possessions – we're supposed to just give those, or at least 10% of them. What will Jesus be stealing from us when he comes again? Our sin? Our guilt about our sin? Suffering? Pain? Death?

OK, I wouldn't be surprised if by this point you are wondering if I am perhaps taking this "thief" image a bit too literally, and maybe I am. Maybe. But I find the implications of this analogy of Jesus coming like a thief in the night unsettling. Again, I think I understand at least generally what Jesus is trying to convey here – that when the Son of Man comes again it will be unexpected and that's why we are warned to watch and wait and stay awake and be prepared. And that, right there, sums up the season of Advent. Advent is not meant to be the comfortable season we have turned it into. We have made Advent into a season that gives us time to attend a few more parties, wrap a few more gifts, send out those Christmas letters, and have some extra shopping days to get ready for Christmas - a time of tinsel and hot chocolate and cookies. But Advent is meant to be a time of waiting and preparing, and a time perhaps when we're supposed to be a little unsettled, on our toes, alert; not sitting back being comfortable and complacent. Above all this reading and its unsettling images reminds us that that's what this whole season of Advent is really about - being a little unsettled, recognizing that the coming of Jesus can be a little disturbing, slightly uncertain, entirely unexpected – like a flood that we're not quite sure when it's going to hit, or a kidnapping that might happen suddenly, or a thief who might break in at any moment. Maybe we are supposed to feel a little unsettled as we start this season of Advent.

So how did I do – are you feeling a little unsettled?

Well if so, Happy Advent!

Amen.

III. Reflections on the Lord's Prayer

Our Heavenly Father
Matthew 7:7-11; James 1:2-5, 12-18

June 7, 2015

Today is the first in a series of sermons I will be preaching this summer considering the Lord's Prayer and what it means in detail, line-by-line. This prayer is important to us partly because it was taught by Jesus. Jesus taught it to his disciples, and to us, both as a prayer we should pray but also as a model and an example of prayer to be followed in all our prayers. Learning about prayer from Jesus himself is sort of like learning how to hit a baseball from Babe Ruth or Ted Williams or learning how to paint from Van Gogh or Picasso – pick someone who is the best in their field and if they told you how to do that thing, you'd be wise to listen. Likewise when Jesus advises us how to pray.

This prayer is one we use so often, every Sunday in worship, at many church events and occasions, and I suspect many of you, like me, use this as your "go to" personal prayer as well. The problem with something so familiar is that we can get so used to saying the words that we stop paying attention to what the words mean. So in these sermons I will be examining what this prayer says, what the words mean, and what we are saying each and every time we pray this prayer that Jesus taught us.

This morning I want to start, oddly enough I know, at the beginning - with the opening of the Lord's Prayer. Our Westminster Confession of Faith calls it the "prelude" of the prayer or the address; we are taught to start this prayer as we might start a letter, if anyone writes letters anymore: "Dear God" or as we say in this prayer, "Our Father, who art in heaven." Six seemingly simple little words. But what do they mean? Why did Jesus teach us that this was an appropriate way to begin a prayer?

The very first word is "Our." I find it interesting that this basic model for prayer taught by Jesus does not start with the word "my" – "My Father." No, Jesus teaches us to start our prayers with "our" - plural, not singular, communal, not individual. As the author and theologian William Barclay noted, the use of this one little word "ends all exclusiveness." Our Father – not "mine" - God is not my private God, not my personal possession - God is ours, God is for all of us. And even if we pray this prayer alone, all by ourselves, in the privacy of our own room, we acknowledge that we are praying to a communal, inclusive God who belongs to all people, to anyone who prays this prayer. This one little word, the very first word of this prayer, not only tells us about our relationship with God, it also declares something about our relationship with every other human being. Because if God is "our Father," that means every single person in the world is a child of this heavenly Father, and also our family member. One little word already tells us all of that.

Now let's consider the word "father." Here we get into some controversy. This word can be controversial for two reasons. One, because it is gender specific. Fathers, at least biologically, are males. Of course that is not what this prayer is saying, let's be clear about that – this prayer is not asserting that God is male or female, or any gender variation in between. It is worth noting that the Bible refers to God as "mother" as well. But also this word "father" for some people can produce some bad associations, because some people have grown up with bad fathers – fathers who have abandoned their children, or abused them, and if that has been someone's experience, addressing God as "father" can raise issues for them.

So let's be clear what Jesus is saying by using this word in this prayer. What he is saying is that God embodies all the qualities of the ideal father, fatherhood at its best and most perfect. Regardless of whether we grew up with good or bad or just neutral father figures in our lives, I'll bet we all would come up with some pretty similar qualities that make for a good father - Strength paired with gentleness; love and affection; someone who provides children what they need, if not always what they want; someone who disciplines bad behavior, but with mercy and forgiveness, not harshness. The list could go on. The noted Quaker author and theologian Elton Trueblood summed it up nicely: *"The best mark, even of an earthly father, is not that he is strong or resourceful or creative, but that he **cares.**"* So when we pray the word "father," I think we are to consider not just our own experience of a father-figure in our lives – an uncle, a grandfather, maybe a teacher or maybe not even a male, perhaps your mother - but the ideal of "father-ness" that God embodies. It might not even be a real person - you might think of Gregory Peck as Atticus Finch in "To Kill a Mockingbird." But whatever qualities you think that ideal father figure, the ideal parent, possesses, those are the qualities God possesses, as we acknowledge every time we pray "our Father."

God loves us - that's what this word "father" ultimately reminds us – God loves us as any good parent loves their child. And God's love is undeserved and unconditional. Undeserved and unconditional love simply because of the relationship, the fact of being a child of our heavenly Father. Also a love that is practical, that is part of everyday life and deals with everyday concerns and needs. Out of God's love for us, God gives us what we need, not just spiritual gifts but all gifts - food, shelter, clothing, family, community, purpose – God provides us what we need to live and flourish, as any good father does. God is the one who gives all good gifts, above and beyond even the best earthly father. Jesus uses the example, almost laughable, in our reading from Matthew's gospel: "Which of you, if your son asks for bread, will give him a stone? Or if he asks for a fish, will give him a snake?" He goes on: "If you, then, though you are evil known how to give good gifts to your children, how much more will your Father in heaven give good gifts to those who ask him." God's love for us and goodness to us as our Father, father of us all, is above and beyond any earthly parent.

Continuing along these lines, the word "father" gets even more interesting. Because the Greek word used here is "Abba" – not to be confused with the Swedish rock band of the 70s. The Greek word "Abba" means more than "father." I'll let William Barclay explain the nuance of this word: *"This word abba is more than father. It was the word by which a little child in Palestine addressed his father in the home circle...There is only one possible English translation of this word in any ordinary use of it, and that is 'Daddy.'"* "Abba" is a term of intimacy and deep trust. Our Father...Our Daddy...Our Papa. That's how intimate this address that begins this prayer is.

And then that description that follows: "who art in heaven" makes this all the more amazing. Because we are reminded that this Being, we are already calling "Daddy" also happens to be Divine. God is the most powerful, awesome, mysterious Being in existence, and yet in this prayer, even as we acknowledge that, we also address God by one of the most intimate of names. This Being whose power and existence we can hardly even imagine, we call "Abba," "Daddy" as we begin this prayer. It is a pretty incredible, almost mind-boggling, way to begin a prayer. And yet that is the model Jesus offers us: to address the Creator of the entire universe in personal, intimate terms as we pour out our hearts in prayer.

Let me again quote William Barclay, who wrote a wonderful book all about the Lord's Prayer: *"Every time we pray, "Our Father," we can know for certain that for God no one is lost in the crowd; that is we matter to no one else, we matter to God; that if no one else cares for us, God cares. Here is something to lift up our hearts every time we pray our Lord's prayer."*

Six simple little words begin this prayer that Jesus taught us to pray. Words that we have probably rushed past time and time again. But I would suggest that these six words teach us some of the most powerful and profound truths we can know about our God and ourselves.

"Our Father, who art in heaven..."

Amen.

The Coming Kingdom
Luke 17:20-21; John 18:33-37

July 5, 2015

"Thy kingdom come."

I have to warn you – this morning's sermon is political.

It has to be, because of those three words we will be considering. "Thy kingdom come" is a political statement. By saying, and praying, those three words, we find ourselves in the midst of a power struggle, which is really what politics is, after all – a struggle for power and control.

"Thy kingdom come." We are praying about God's kingdom. And by praying that, we are setting it against all other kingdoms...and nations and countries and institutions and powers of this world, all earthly kingdoms. God's kingdom is different than the kingdoms and nations and countries of this world. It is worth noting before we go on that the gospels talk about the "kingdom of God" and the "kingdom of heaven" both, and they are synonymous terms - Matthew tends to use "kingdom of heaven" and the other gospels tend to say "kingdom of God," but they mean roughly the same thing. The thing about God's kingdom is you can't point to it, it's not a physical location or a place. Any earthly kingdom or country or nation, even if they have shifting boundaries, still has boundaries, it can be pointed to. I remember a class in high school called "World Affairs," in which we had to learn every single country and how to identify it on a world map. Of course, much of that knowledge is now out of date – a distressingly large number of countries whose names I learned back then no longer exist or have changed their name. God's kingdom is different than earthly kingdoms and countries and nations. You can't point to it – actually you can't NOT point to it – because it is everywhere. It has no boundary. "The kingdom of God" is not a reference to a place at all; it is a reference to the entire reign of God – which is everywhere, everyone, everything. The reign of God encompasses ALL. That's the kingdom of God. It is everything, everywhere, in every time. So the kingdom of God is unlike any earthly kingdoms, which are always bound to a particular time and place and boundary.

So here's where things get political. We say to God "Thy kingdom come" - your kingdom come, God. And by saying that we acknowledge who is in charge, we acknowledge where our loyalty lies, we acknowledge where we place our ultimate trust. Not in any earthly kingdom, or power, or person, or party, or institution, or nation, but in God's kingdom. That's a pretty radical thing to say, as a human being living here on earth, in a particular country, with all sorts of memberships and affiliations with human institutions. Maybe especially on Independence Day weekend. As Christians living in the United States of America, our ultimate allegiance is to God, and God's kingdom. That's where our ultimate hope lies.

Christians are, I believe, to be involved in the life of their own country. We are to vote, even to run for office, and to work for change in our country and in the institutions, we are part of, but always with the perspective that any change is always temporary and limited. The result of any election, no matter how sweeping, for good or for ill, is always temporary and limited in scope. I love election season. I take great pride in voting, and I vote in every election, whether national, state, local, or for neighborhood dog catcher. I love reading the history of the United States, especially political history and biography – I find all this fascinating. But…more and more I realize that it all falls short ultimately. Ultimate Truth lies elsewhere. We work for change, but we know that true change and transformation comes from God; we celebrate July 4th, Independence Day, and the ideals and principles upon which this nation was founded, but we acknowledge that true independence and freedom comes from God, not from any human institution or government.

Are you beginning to see how radical those three little words are: "thy kingdom come"? Not our country, not our political party, not any institution of our making, but YOUR kingdom come, O God. This is a radical statement of allegiance to a kingdom above and beyond anything on earth.

I'm pretty sure that in God's kingdom there are no flags, no statues, no monuments, no political parties, no debates – none of the trappings of modern nations and politics. Well, maybe parades. I'll bet there are some pretty awesome parades in heaven. In God's kingdom there is just God…and all of us. Living together, being together, enjoying life together. Nothing else to get in the way. And no calories or fat, either…but's that's getting a little off point. Doesn't that sound nice, though?

God – your kingdom come. That's our ultimate hope. Even as we work to make this world reflect, to some degree, God's kingdom, we know that it never will, ultimately - it will always be a pale reflection at best, as if seen through a mirror, dimly, until Christ comes again.

Which gets us to the third point about these three little words: "thy kingdom come." We pray about a kingdom that is not yet, yet we pray for it to "come". When the Pharisees in Luke chapter 17 ask Jesus about God's kingdom, they ask: "When is God's kingdom coming?" I suspect they'd like Jesus to give them a specific date. So many people throughout history have tried to pinpoint the exact date when the world will end, or, if they are Christian, when Jesus will come again. October 22, 1844; January 1, 2000; December 21, 2012. Every single person who has ever predicted the exact date for the end of the world has, so far, always been absolutely, 100%, wrong. But an exact date for the coming of God's kingdom is not what Jesus is concerned about or interested in preaching. Jesus says in reply, "I'm not going to give you a day and time, but I can tell you that the signs of God's kingdom are not easily noticed, and it will not come when you expect. In fact, you've been so busy predicting dates and looking for signs that you've missed this important fact: God's kingdom is already among you."

Now this is true on many levels. For one thing Jesus is saying, "God's kingdom has come, because I am here." Jesus is the embodiment of God's kingdom. The minute Jesus was born there in Bethlehem God's kingdom arrived on earth. And yet Jesus teaches us to pray: "Thy kingdom come." So obviously God's kingdom is not fully here yet. Jesus did the work that he had to do (and Mary, too, let's not forget her part in bringing God's kingdom in the form of Jesus into the world). But there is still work that remains to be done, before God's kingdom is fully realized, before it comes in all its glory and goodness before that coming is complete. Jesus planted the seed; Jesus made God's kingdom take root in the soil of this world and our lives, but now we await the full bearing of the fruit of the kingdom. Each and every time we pray "Thy kingdom come," we are saying that the kingdom is here among us, but not yet fully realized, which means that maybe there's still work for us to do.

These three little words at the beginning of this familiar prayer are all about change. When you pray "Thy kingdom come," you are, whether you realize it or not, praying that God will help you be open to being transformed and changed yourself. Yes, we pray that our world might be transformed and changed, but that prayer includes us as well. This is not a prayer that celebrates the status quo. This is not a prayer that says: "Let's go back to an earlier time when everything, at least in our memories, was wonderful and ideal." These three little words remind us that God's kingdom is still not yet fully here, which means there is some change that must occur before it does. They also acknowledge that we recognize that we have a part in helping bring about that change, in some way, that we each have our role to play and our tasks to perform.

Let me conclude with some words from William Barclay, one of our guides through this sermon series. Here is what Barclay says, in the slightly anachronistic language of his time, about these three little words and their meaning when we pray them: *"The Kingdom of God will come. Secretly, silently, but unstoppable the seed grows. Man can delay the Kingdom and man can hinder the Kingdom, but in the end the Kingdom will come."* He goes on to say this: *"No man need pray this prayer unless he is prepared to hand himself over to the grace of Gods in order that that grace may make him a new creature. This is no prayer for the man who desires to stay the way he is."*

Because of these three little words, "Thy kingdom come," this is no prayer for a community that desires to stay the way it is, either. Three little words. Did you ever realize what a radical political statement you are making every time you pray them?

"Thy kingdom come."

To us…

In us…

Through us.

Today…and every day after that.

Amen.

Offering Up Our Will
Psalm 40; Matthew 26:36-42

July 12, 2015

As we continue our journey through the Lord's Prayer, we have reached that petition in this prayer that I would suggest is sometimes the hardest one to say and truly mean.

"Thy will be done."

Not mine. Not yours. Not ours. But God's will be done.

William Barclay suggests a number of possible emotional states in which one can pray this phrase - he remarks that it is possible to pray "Thy will be done" in a tone of bitter resentment, through clenched teeth perhaps, "I don't like it, but go ahead God, give it your best shot, thy will be done." Bitter acceptance of God's will. It is said of the composer Ludwig Beethoven, who struggled and battled against his own deafness, that when he was found dead "his fists where clenched and his lips drawn back in a snarl," as if raging to the bitter end against God and life and fate. You can pray "Thy will be done" in that spirit, in that tone – bitter and resentful and defiant.

You can pray this phrase simply with a sense of resignation, almost indifference. "Whatever, God, just do whatever you want." Sort of the way you might get with your family after 20 minutes of discussing where to go eat dinner that night: "I don't care, just somebody make a decision." You can pray it in that tone, that mood. "God, you just make the decision, do your will, I don't really care."

And then there is at least a third way in which to pray this phrase, and that is with "serene and trustful love." Not with bitterness, not with resignation, but with a sense of joy, and peace. To trust that God will do the right thing, that God works all things ultimately for good. And not to be resistant or resigned to God's will, but to embrace it, to even find joy and peace in knowing God is in charge.

Of course that can be tougher than it sounds. That's why I began saying this phrase may be to hardest part of the Lord's Prayer to say and truly mean. Because to pray to God: "Thy will be done," means we have to give up our way and our will and our illusion that we are in control. Most of life is out of our control, but we like to fool ourselves into thinking otherwise. "Thy will be done" ruptures that illusion. And it reminds us that the main thing we have control over in life is our own behavior and our own reaction to things that happen. Most everything else is entirely out of our control. To pray "Thy will be done" is to say, "I'm giving up any illusion that I'm in control of things; that my will, my hope, is the final word." And for some of us, maybe all of us at times, that can be difficult to say, and to do. We like to think we ARE in control, or that we have if not all at least some of the answers. To pray "Thy will be done" is to acknowledge that God is in charge, not me. That God's will takes precedence, not mine. It is to let go of our sense of how things ought to be.

Look, I have my opinions about a lot of issues. "I know exactly what to do about the Confederate flag issue and racism and about dealing with ISIS and terrorism and the immigration issue. It's too bad that no one is asking me because I have all the answers." This is the Donald Trump view of things – just elect me and I will solve all your problems. I know exactly what to do, and I'm the only one who does and can make it happen. Over and against that view of the world, when we pray "Thy will be done," we are acknowledging that we don't have all the answers, that none of us has a lock on Truth, that we are not in charge of the universe, God is. It is a phrase of great humility. It means we have to acknowledge that our way, our desire for how we want things to go, may not be the best way. "God, I don't see the end of the path, I don't know all the answers, I'm not sure I have the strength or courage to even face or contemplate the next twist and turn of the journey of life, so I'm putting all my trust in you, God, and in your good and loving and gracious will."

Now another difficulty with praying "Thy will be done" and meaning it, is it also means we have to learn to be patient, which may be even harder than learning humility and giving up the illusion of control. To pray "Thy will be done" is to leave the outcome, and the timing of that outcome, to God...and then to wait. And keep waiting. I'm reminded of that famous prayer: "God grant me patience and give it to me right now." I'm also reminded of one of my favorite knock-knock jokes:

Knock-knock

Who's there?

Impatient cow.

Impatient cow wh—MOO!

[I didn't say it was a good knock-knock joke, just one of my favorites]

Some of us are like impatient cows, we are not very good at being patient. But when we pray "Thy will be done," we are asking God to help us be patient, to wait for God's will to be done. Did you notice our Psalm this morning, Psalm 40, begins with a line about waiting: "I waited patiently for the Lord?" God, you may not act in the way I want or expect. You may not act as quickly as I'd like. But I am leaving all that up to you, God. That can be a tough thing to pray and to mean. Because we have to give up control, we have to be patient.

The third thing I want to suggest about this phrase: "Thy will be done," is that it is also a statement about peace and contentment. Because when, maybe I should say "if," we get to the point where we can truly give things over to God, to rely solely on God's will, it can be an incredible comfort to give that control over to God. It means we can let go of the often-overwhelming weight of anxiety and worry and fear that comes from us trying to carry the whole weight of the world ourselves. The promise in Scripture is that God works all things for good, ultimately. Especially if we can get out of the way. We can be our own worst enemies sometimes. God working all things for good does not mean things will always go the way we want them to go. God sees the whole sweep of time and of events – beginning, middle, and end. God knows that the decisions that can seem good to us in the moment, can sometimes not turn out so well in the end. So if we can truly say to God: "Thy will be done," we leave ourselves open to that goodness of God's will and God's power, working all things, even seemingly bad, awful things, ultimately for good. As Julian of Norwich so famously asserted over and over again: "All will be well, and all manner of things will be well." Maybe not right now, or today, or even in the foreseeable future, but someday, in God's time, in God's will. That's why it is wise to let God handle the world, to let God be in charge, and to trust that God knows what God is doing, even if we can't quite see it yet. To be at peace, therefore, in praying "Thy will be done."

And Jesus not only taught us to pray this, and prayed it himself, but "Thy will be done" might have been the very core of Jesus's life and work. Jesus said it repeatedly: "I have come to do the will of my Father in heaven." And when he finally got to the garden of Gethsemane and he realized he was on the brink of betrayal and arrest and crucifixion and death, and even as he acknowledged he didn't want to experience those things – who would? – he prayed in that moment: "Yet not as I will, but as you will." "Thy will be done." Since we got started today with the help of William Barclay, let me end with another quote from him to conclude: *"Jesus prayer to be released from his ordeal, but only if it should be the will of God. He was not released; but he was given the power to go through it. When we pray, "Thy will be done," we are not praying for release; we are not praying for resignation; we are praying for triumph. We are praying not to be taken out of a situation, but to be enabled to face it and conquer it and defeat it."*

It's a tough one, but if we can learn to not only pray "Thy will be done," but mean it, and live it, that is the beginning, at least, of the road leading to true peace.

Amen.

Heavenly Action

Isaiah 6:1-8; Matthew 21:28-32

July 19, 2015

"On earth as it is in heaven."

Since I have been considering phrases of the Lord's Prayer rather than complete sentences, it is worth noting that today's phrase is the completion of the sentence that begins: "Thy will be done," but also, I'd suggest, the completion of all the opening petitions of this prayer. What we are saying here is: "God, hallowed be thy name...on earth as it is in heaven. Thy kingdom come...on earth as it is in heaven. Thy will be done...on earth as it is in heaven." May all these things be done here on earth as they are done in heaven.

The Bible gives us a number of snapshots of what heaven might be like – we read one of them here in Isaiah 6 – and our Thursday morning Bible study has been reading through the Book of Revelation, which is full of snapshots and pictures of heaven. And there are numerous others in Scripture. All of them agree on at least this one thing about heaven: heaven is a place where there is constant worship of God. And we're not talking long boring earthly worship services, this is not the sort of "worship" during which you keep looking at your watch or glancing at your cellphone – remember, you've got eternity in heaven, you've got all the time in the world plus I'm not even sure there are watches and cellphones in heaven. But the larger point is that worship in heaven, hallowing God's name, glorifying God, praising God won't be boring and tedious and time consuming like it unfortunately can be here on earth. You won't have any desire to just stay in bed and worship St. Mattress of the Springs instead of going to church. Every moment will be worship, and it will be glorious and wonderful and exciting, partly because God will be RIGHT THERE with you as you worship, and what could be better than that? But to get back to the prayer – in addition to worship, God's will is done perfectly in heaven, and God's kingdom has already come, perfectly and wonderfully, in heaven. That's what we say in this phrase "on earth as it is in heaven." May all this that is done perfectly in heaven be reflected to some degree on earth.

Which begs the question: Is that even possible? Is it possible for this world to reflect in any way what goes on in heaven? I've been pondering the news about the shooting in Chattanooga recently, especially since it personally affected a member of this congregation. And that is just one of the news items throughout the week that hit me in considering this question. We read and hear about violence and hatred and animosity and death and hunger and suffering, and I think at times, if we're honest, we might begin to wonder: "What's the point? Where's the hope?" Everything in the news always seems bad, negative, awful, even. Is it even possible for this earth, full of human beings who so often do so many awful things, to reflect any aspect of heaven; for there to be love and joy and hope and peace here on earth, reflecting what goes on in heaven?

Well, every time we pray the Lord's Prayer and we pray "on earth as it is in heaven," we are saying that we still believe it IS possible. "On earth as it IS in heaven" is a prayer of hope, the hope that somehow, someway, earth can reflect heaven. We are saying we still believe, despite all the evidence showing otherwise, no matter how bad things get, no matter how incomprehensibly bad the behavior of human beings may be at times, it is still possible for earth to reflect the values of heaven. We acknowledge that every time we pray this prayer.

Scottish theologian and pastor David H. C. Read challenges us this way: *"But what about us? Do we still believe that the life we know on this earth – our own baffled and mixed-up lives, the fearful confusions, dangers, diseases, and hostilities of the world around us – can in any way be moved towards the perfection of God's design? Is there really any possibility of edging this earth nearer heaven? Can you and I be better people? Can our church, our city, our nation, our generation around the world be moved closer to the kingdom? If we don't really think this is possible, we had better give up this prayer."*

So if we believe it is indeed possible for earth to reflect heaven, this leads to the next question: How? This brings us back to Isaiah, the prophet who is given a vision of heaven. At the end of Isaiah's vision, God says to the angels and the saints gathered there: "Whom shall we send?" Who will go and do our heavenly work back on earth? Who can we find to help make earth reflect heaven? And this is the moment when I picture Isaiah swallowing loudly and glancing around and maybe waiting for someone else to step forward and then finally meekly raising his hand and saying, in a still small voice perhaps: "Well…um…here I am. Um…send me. I'll go."

If earth is to in any way reflect heaven, it will only happen if we each realize we have a role to play in making it so. We each are called to do our part. Jesus tells this parable in Matthew's gospel about two sons being asked by their father to go work in the vineyard. The first son says: "No way, Pop. I've got better things to do," and I think his initial refusal is not just because he doesn't want to, I think he may have real doubts about whether he can even do the work his father is asking him to do. "I don't know if I can do that work, I'm not sure, I don't know a weed from a vine, I haven't been trained in vineyard management." So the first son refuses, initially. But upon reflection, despite whatever doubts or fears or uncertainties or even seemingly better offers he may have, he goes to the vineyard and works for his father. Now the second son says all the right things, all the things you'd want to hear from a seemingly obedient child: "You bet, Dad. I'll be right there; I'll get right on it. Your wish is my command." But he never actually goes to the vineyard. This reminds me a bit of the many Christians who wear their religion on their sleeve, who say all the right things, whose every other word is "Jesus," Jesus-this and Jesus-that, and who wear crosses and carry Bibles and make sure everyone can see that they are Christians, but if you watch what they actually DO in their daily lives, how they treat other people, you might never know they are followers of Christ. They act nice for an hour on Sunday mornings, but then the rest of the week they are gossiping and negative and snarling at everyone they meet, kicking dogs and stealing candy from babies. They say the right things when they know people are listening, but it turns out to all be for show. Their behavior doesn't match their words. They don't practice what they preach. That's the second son. He says the right thing, but he doesn't actually go and do the work. I fear I fall into this camp more often than I'd care to admit (*Let's just keep that our little secret, OK?*). Even the Pharisees, when asked by Jesus which of these sons really did the will of his father know the right answer, it is so obvious: the first son. The son who doesn't say the right words, who doesn't even appear to be on board, but who goes and does the work.

If earth is to reflect heaven it is up to us and it will only happen through our actions. Not just on Sunday mornings but every single moment of the week. And I'm not talking about big grand earth-shattering actions here, I'm talking about the small, everyday gestures and behaviors and habits we perform. Mustard seed actions that look so small but can grow so large. A smile instead of a frown. A kind word instead of a criticism. A hug, a pat on the shoulder, an encouraging word rather than crossing the street to avoid someone who might slow down our journey. Just being with someone at a low point, a stressful moment, not with fancy poetic words but with the heartfelt silence of being present. Small things, that, if everyone does them, could indeed change the world and make it more like heaven.

"Thy will be done on earth, as it is in heaven" … and let it begin with me.

Amen.

Our Daily Bread

Deuteronomy 8:1-18; John 6:26-35, 49-58

July 26, 2015

"Give us this day our daily bread."

In some ways this sentence represents the very heart and soul of the Lord's Prayer. And I want to consider in some detail what this seemingly simple and straightforward sentence really means and what we are saying when we pray it. The core of this petition is: bread. Give us bread. That simple phrase leaves itself open for a wide array of uses. As we are reminded by theologian Helmut Thielicke, *"It can be said by a child, praying for bread and butter and it can also be uttered in that agonizing zone between 'annihilation and survival'."* There are many interpretations of this phrase because there are many meanings to the word "bread."

Let's start with the most obvious one – this is a prayer for physical food and physical needs. This is a reminder that our God supplies our most basic daily human needs. Food. Water. Shelter. Clothing. Good book to read. God cares about our bodies and about our physical and mental well-being. God is not just an abstract entity "up there" somewhere, distant and detached from us. God is involved in our everyday lives, providing for our most basic needs. That's why God sent manna to the Israelites when they were wandering in the wilderness for 40 years – God provided them with something to eat. Well, OK, maybe he was also getting tired of their complaining about not having anything to eat, but that's for another sermon. This miraculous bread would appear on the ground, like dew, every morning. And not only that, to provide some variety, and, yet again, to quiet their complaining, God also sent flocks of quail that would land right inside the camp, right outside their tents. Home delivery. Just walk outside your

119

tent, and there's your meal – Pluck & Eat (the Israelites probably grumbled that the quail didn't come pre-plucked, but that's for another sermon). The point is, God supplies our basic needs. God knows them and provides for them. "Give us this day our daily bread." And so God gives us bread. God doesn't promise us filet mignon or duck pate or chocolate mousse, nor do we ask for luxuries like that – we ask simply for bread. As Gregory of Nyssa preached in the 4th century, we don't pray for delicacies or riches or magnificent purple robes or golden ornaments or precious stones or silver dishes but only for bread, the simple necessity of life. Give us what we need this day, to survive – and God gives it.

When we pray: "Give us this day our daily bread," we are asking for spiritual food as well. As Moses reminds the people in Deuteronomy "man does not live on bread alone but on every word that comes from the mouth of the Lord." So we pray for and God provides for us spiritual nourishment as well as physical food. "Feed us, God – spiritually. Give us the time and the inclination to turn to your Word, to say some prayers, to worship and be fed by your presence and your grace. Give us a community where we can be fed and nurtured and supported as well, one that will nourish us along our journey of faith." We are reminded of communion, the Lord's Supper, when we pray this phrase – that sharing of bread and juice that remind us of God's love and God's presence; a physical piece of bread that offers spiritual sustenance in that particular context. And that leads us to perhaps the most important aspect of "bread," the "bread of life" – Jesus. This is the controversy Jesus finds himself in in the 6th chapter of John's gospel when he describes himself as the "true bread from heaven," and the people start to take offense: "What's he talking about? Are we supposed to eat his flesh, like cannibals?" And Jesus says, "well, sort of, yes – eat of me, all of you." What Jesus is saying is that he has come to give us "life," and that he is the very real presence of the God of Life, and when we eat of that bread, we find salvation. Not just physical food, not just spiritual comfort, but salvation and eternal life. Salvation from ourselves and our appetites and desires and bad behaviors. All of this is wrapped up in that little word, "bread." "Give us our daily bread."

In other words, give us everything we need. And notice we say: "Give us this DAY our DAILY bread." This prayer asks for what we need for that particular day, one day at a time. Remember that it was Jesus who said: "Don't worry about tomorrow." Focus on today. Once again remember that manna that God provided each and every morning (except on the Sabbath) there in the wilderness. The instruction from God was this: "Gather just enough for each day, but no more." But, being human, the Israelites got out their Tupperware containers and took extra to save for the next day - you know, just in case. But when they took more than they needed for that day, the extra manna would rot and get wormy. God promised: "Rely on me, I will provide each and every day enough for that day." So we are told by Jesus to pray for our "daily bread," to be given to us "this day," and then we'll pray again when tomorrow comes. Give me what I need today, and when tomorrow becomes today, I'll pray again for bread for that day.

The truly brilliant aspect of this phrase which asks for God to give us today our daily bread is that we are thus encouraged to pray this prayer each and every day. If Jesus had taught us instead to pray: "Give us this week our weekly bread," we wouldn't have the incentive to pray it every single day. But since Jesus so cleverly teaches us to pray for our daily bread, he encourages us to pray as a daily practice. Pretty smart guy, that Jesus.

And notice we pray "GIVE us." We rely on God to give us what we need each and every day, we trust that God will indeed give to us what we need. God the one, the only one, who can truly provide us what we need, give us our daily bread and everything we need for today. But this is also a call for us to be ready to receive what God will give, and to be ready to receive it each and every day, just as God gives it. This phrase is a call to action, the action of having open hands and open hearts, ready to receive what God so freely and lovingly gives.

And finally, as with the opening of the Lord's Prayer, notice the plural pronoun used in this phrase. We pray "give US this day OUR daily bread." Now who's the "us"? Well it's not just me, and it's not just you. We don't say "give all Presbyterians this day their daily bread," or "all Democrats," or "all Republicans" or "all Americans" or even "all Christians." We say, "give us." Who's "us"? Everyone. Every single human being, maybe every single living creature in the world. "Give us – give everyone – their daily bread." All of us. No exceptions. As with the opening address to "Our Father," even if you are praying this prayer all by yourself, you are praying it on behalf of everyone.

So notice what this simple phrase really says: "God, give everyone in the world today everything they need to get them through the day." That pretty much covers it, doesn't it? In that sense, you really don't need any other prayer than that. "Give everyone in the world everything they need from you today, God." Have you ever found yourself talking to someone who is having a particularly rough time and you don't know what to say or even how to begin praying for them? Well, here you go: "Give this person today their daily bread, whatever they need. Because you know what they need, God, even if I don't." This phrase could be the summation of our Prayers of the People every single Sunday in worship: "Give us this day our daily bread." It takes care of, and covers, everything, really…by lifting it up to God and God's daily care.

I want to conclude by quoting something that the Scottish preacher and theologian David H. C. Read wrote about this phrase, particularly the word "us": *"In the mind of Jesus, "us" has one vast, inclusive meaning. It is the whole family of mankind. When you kneel, after a day in which your own bodily needs have been cared for – and say, "Give us each day our daily bread," your prayer not only reminds you of your plenty; it is for the feeding of that family, perhaps not so far away, where there are too many mouths for the food available; for that emaciated boy sleeping on the streets of Calcutta; for that woman up in the Andes who has nothing for her children tomorrow; for all whom Jesus teaches us to remember in this prayer. "Give us this day our daily bread!" – we are joining in the cry of the family to which we belong. And, as with every prayer that Jesus prompts, there must be action to follow. Could you sit down with a hungry man before a loaf of bread, say grace, and then eat the whole of it yourself?"*

When we pray: "Give us this day our daily bread," we acknowledge that we are looking to God to supply our every need, we are looking to God to supply everyone's every need, and we are also saying that we are ready to do our little part to further that effort as well. It seems like such a simple little phrase, doesn't it? But these few simple words reveal profound truths and profound responsibilities for each one of us.

Amen.

Our Debtors

Matthew 18:21-35; Colossians 3:12-14

August 9, 2015

"Forgive us our debts as we forgive our debtors."

Last week I offered some reflections about "our debts" and the ways we are indebted to ourselves, to other people, and to God.

That was the easy part.

"As we forgive our debtors." The crux of the matter for this week is this little word "as," and its placement in the sentence. How I wish Jesus had reversed the order of this sentence when teaching us the Lord's Prayer. I wish Jesus had taught us to pray: "Help us to forgive our debtors as you forgive our debts." That would be a lot easier. That would say "God, as you forgive us, help us to forgive others in the same way." But that's not what the Lord's Prayer says. It says, "Forgive us our debts AS we forgive our debtors." It is conditional, with the main condition being placed on us. This is similar to what Jesus says at the end of the parable about the unforgiving servant in Matthew 18. Jesus say the moral of this parable is - and Jesus didn't often tell people what he thought the moral of a parable was, he left them to figure it out for themselves, so this is unusual – Jesus says the moral of the parable is, "this is how your heavenly Father will treat you UNLESS you forgive your brothers and sisters from your heart."

"AS we forgive our debtors...UNLESS you forgive your brother and sister from your heart..." These are conditional statements. What's being suggested in the Lord's Prayer and in this parable is that if we are not forgiving of others, God may not forgive us; that God's divine forgiveness may depend upon our willingness and ability to forgive. These things – our forgiveness and God's forgiveness, are tied closely together. And the warning is – if we are not forgiving, we are putting in jeopardy God's forgiveness of us.

This is an old idea. It grows out of the Jewish tradition that our Christian faith grows out of. The great Jewish teacher of the first century, Gamaliel, said this: "So long as you are merciful, God will have mercy upon you, and if you are not merciful, he will not be merciful to you." And another great Jewish teacher suggested that God forgives the person "who overlooks the transgressions of others," and then added, "So long as a man remains in his stiffness God does not forgive him." It seems that God's forgiveness of us is conditional and depends upon how well we forgive others. That's tough to hear, that's a rather troubling thought, isn't it?

But it does make sense. Gregory of Nyssa in one of his famous sermons on the Lord's Prayer in the 4th century stated that this had to be because there can be no fellowship between opposites, especially when it comes to our relationship with God. In other words, if we are not forgiving, if we are, as Gregory says, "callous" or "merciless," there is no way we can have fellowship with, be in relationship with, a loving, merciful God. If we are unable to forgive others, we cut ourselves off from our forgiving God. If we are not loving, we cut ourselves off from our loving God. This is our choice, not God's. We can be connected and in fellowship with God by trying – trying, mind you – to be like God, or we can choose to sever that relationship and that bond. "Forgive us our debts AS WE forgive our debtors." You see, it's in God's nature to want to be with creatures that are like God.

We humans can never truly be like God, but we can choose to move in that direction. If we pray the Lord's Prayer, and this phrase "forgive us our debts as we forgive our debtors," and we do so not having forgiven all of your debtors, all those holding something against us, we are in essence praying for God NOT to forgive us. "Forgive us our debts as we forgive our debtors," and if we haven't forgiven our debtors when we pray this, then we are praying for God to not forgive us and bringing judgment upon ourselves.

But…there IS good news, as there always is with God. If we can make the effort, if we can begin to move in the direction of being forgiving - and I do believe it is very much about our intention, about the attempt on our part, because God knows better than to expect perfection from us – if we can try to forgive our debtors, if we can begin to forgive those we feel owe us some sort of debts, and forgive "debts" against us, and do it truly from our hearts, with honest intent to be forgiving, then we will begin to become more and more, bit by bit, like God, or at least like the people God wants us to be, the sort of people who CAN be in relationship with God.

You may remember that sometimes when Jesus would heal people in the gospels, he would also tell them, "your sins are forgiven." This would enrage the Pharisees of his day, they would say: "Who can forgive sins but God?" Hmmm. Well, WE can. And even if it is true that only God can forgive sins, that means when we forgive sins and forgive our debtors, we become a little more like God, to whatever extent that is possible. As we strive to forgive and to be forgiving - because forgiveness is not a "one-time" deal, it is a continuing way of behaving, you have to keep being forgiving – as difficult as it is, we move ever closer to God, ever closer to being a little more like God. And that's a pretty amazing thing to consider, isn't it? A way we humans can become a little more like God.

It was mentioned already this morning in our prayers that we are remembering the 70th anniversary of the dropping of the atomic bombs on Japan, a reminder that we live in a world full of war, full of violence, a world that involves retribution and vengeance and "if you hurt me, I'll hurt you," or even "I'd better hurt you first before you can hurt me," and we see this in world affairs and in domestic violence and in our prison system and even in Presidential debates. This very human idea that we've got to hit back, we've got to hit first, go on the offensive as a form of defense, or at least give back as it is given to us. How can there be any hope for us to ever get out of this cycle – this tragic, awful, horrendous cycle – of hurting other people, other nations, how can we ever get out of that mindset if we, as individuals are not trying to be forgiving in our own lives, if we are not willing to try to forgive our debtors? If we cannot forgive the relatively tiny little debts we feel people owe us, what possible chance is there for the Israelis to forgive the Palestinians, and vice-versa, or for the various human races to forgive each other and be forgiven by each other for past sins and deep, deep debts owed, for Democrats and Republicans to forgive their stupid little squabbles and ever get along and work together for the good of the country as a whole? It starts with each of us beginning to forgive our debtors. It must begin with us. There's no other place for reconciliation to start.

So in this nice, comforting, familiar old prayer, that we've been praying all this time, we find the secret to moving closer to God and furthering any possibility of a relationship with God and with each other. By praying it, we are setting the bar pretty high and making it kinda tough on ourselves, but with good reason - for the future survival of the human race.

"Forgive us our debts, as we forgive our debtors." That may be our greatest challenge, and our greatest hope, if we can just learn to do it.

Amen

Tempted!
James 1:12-16; Matthew 4:1-11

August 23, 2015

Before officially jumping into today's sermon, every time I hear this story of the temptation of Jesus I feel I should offer a Public Service Announcement. Notice that one of the profound ironies of that story is that both Jesus and Satan quote Scripture. So, this gives me the opportunity to remind you that just because someone can quote Scripture to you, it does not mean that they are speaking in God's voice.

So having said that, on to TEMPTATION.

What's the first thing you think of when you hear the word "temptation"?

I immediately think of pie. A table full of all kinds of delicious pies – I've never met a pie I didn't like, all varieties, and that includes ala mode, with whipped cream on top. Maybe even a few pizza pies, which I know dates me for even using that term but thrown in for added temptation.

Temptation. "Lead us not into temptation" we pray in this prayer that Jesus taught us.

There are two things I want to focus on this morning, and the first is what we mean when we say "temptation" in this prayer, and the other is what we mean when we pray "lead us not into…" Let me begin by mentioning the Greek word used here for "temptation." The Greek word is *peirasmos*. The general English translation of this word as "temptation" is a bit misleading. *Peirasmos* is a noun, but it doesn't exactly mean "temptation" in the sense of a table full of pies, or whatever you were thinking of a moment ago. That ending, "asmos," always denotes a process, not just a singular event. A better English rendering of this word might be a "test" or a "trial," something that occurs over time, not just once. The verb form of *peirasmos* means "to test" or "to examine," again, giving the sense of something occurring over a period of time, not just in one singular moment. This word is found throughout the Bible. For example, when the apostle Paul writes to the Corinthians the second time and he says to them: "Examine yourselves to see whether you are living in the faith," (*2 Corinthians 13:5*) the word he uses is the verb form of *peirasmos*. Examine and test yourselves, over time not just in one quick moment. So the idea here is not just about a table of pie, it is the idea of an examination or a test over time.

That's certainly what happens to Jesus in the wilderness. He is being tempted, tested, examined even, by Satan. Surrounding this word is the idea of something that entices you, tempts you, over time, more than once - a series of tests. Something that you are tempted to put in place of God. There is a relationship here between the idea of temptation and idolatry, worshipping something in place of God. That's always the way temptation is presented in the Bible – something or someone that shifts our focus away from God. And it doesn't have to be a bad thing – I mean, I think a table full of pie would be awesome. But if whatever it is gets between you and God, that's a problem, that's the temptation. Notice that Jesus is tempted by some not-so-good things, like jumping off the pinnacle of the Temple and trusting in the angels to save him, and they probably would have, but it would still be a pretty silly and dangerous thing to do. Some of us humans are tempted sometimes to do silly and dangerous things, also, but that's for another sermon. Remember that Jesus hasn't eaten for forty days and forty nights, so when Satan tempts him to turn a stone into bread, he's hungry. So what's the problem? Well, as Jesus points out in his reply to Satan, the question is: "Am I relying on my own power, or relying on, and trusting in, God?" That's the temptation – not the bread from a stone, but the reliance on our own power rather than trusting in God. That's the test.

The great Christian writer and theologian Origen, when discussing the book of Job, pointed out that in his opinion all of us face temptation continuously, at almost every moment of our lives. And remember we are talking about this not as a one-time temptation but as a continuing test. According to Origen, every moment of our lives is a test in the sense that we are confronted with choices to make. Are we sticking to God's path and staying in touch with God, or are we letting something else or someone else get in the way?

Temptation is a form of testing. There's a good way to look at this and a not-so-good way. The good way is that temptation in this sense is a test that demonstrates that we are able to withstand it, that strengthens us in the very testing itself. There are references in some of the Psalms to God refining us like steel, forging and tempering us in the fire of testing, rendering us stronger in our faith. That's the positive side of this idea of temptation as testing. It can demonstrate the strength of our faith, most helpfully to ourselves. The not-so-good way is revealed in the fact that the Greek word *peirasmos* can also refer to something that entices us to sin. In other words, we fail the test. That what we are talking about when we pray: "lead us not into temptation" - lead us not into this time of testing and trial Every moment of our lives is a moment of testing and temptation, as Origen said. So let's get away from the verb here and talk about what we are actually praying for when we pray not to be led into temptation.

Again the English is a bit misleading, because the English makes it sounds like we are asking God not to be the one who leads us into temptation, which is a troubling thought - I mean, the idea that otherwise God WOULD be the one leading us into temptation. But I think James is right when he says: "It isn't God who is tempting you...God doesn't do that." I mean, oddly enough, if that's what we're actually saying here – "don't tempt me" – we should be praying this prayer to Satan, not God. But what we're really saying here, according to the original Greek, is "bring us not into the time of temptation," or "allow us not to be brought into a time of trial and testing." Maybe it helps to consider what Saint Augustine said about this phrase: Augustine distinguished between "being tempted" and being "brought into temptation." According to Augustine, sounding a bit like Origen, we all are being tempted, all the time – life is full of temptations, in fact it is a continual series of them. Being brought into temptation for Augustine meant being overpowered and controlled, even subdued, by temptation. So what we are praying is for God to help that NOT to happen.

This is a good point at which to notice what else James says. After saying God isn't the one tempting us, James declares: "one is tempted by one's own desire, being lured and enticed by it." In other words, we tempt ourselves, at least our desires do. It is our own desire, not some mischievous God, who tempts us and lures us and entices us to sin. It is our own desires that lead us astray, what some of the ancient Christian writers called our "passions." So the problem is not the table full of pie, it is my desire to taste them all. We are venturing into the realm of addiction here – the desire for something that just takes control of us, despite our best intentions. Our desire for anything other than God, anything we think might, even fleetingly, makes us happy other than God, can tempt us away from God. Our desire leads us into temptation, and so when we pray: "bring us not into temptation," what we're really saying to God is: "Make sure you go with us and we are not left all alone with our desire." That's what we really are praying – God don't leave us alone here in this world, don't leave us alone with this unsavory-looking desire of ours, but go with us, be with us, all along the journey and keep us safe - from ourselves. Because God, we know we are weak, but you are strong, and only with your guidance and your assistance and under the shelter of your loving care can we prevail over our own desires. But with your help, O God, we can and will prevail, no matter what the test, no matter what the temptation.

Amen.

Deliverance

Psalm 59:1-5, 16-17; Psalm 91

August 30, 2015

"Lead us not into temptation but deliver us from evil."

Last week we considered the first part of this phrase, and I suggested that we're not really talking about one moment of temptation here, but the continuous, lifelong battle against our own desires, against the desire to find happiness in anything other than God. And when we pray for God not to lead us into temptation, we are really asking for God to go with us and help see us through this lifelong battle and not let us be overcome or overpowered by them.

Today I want to consider the second part of this phrase and talk about deliverance. Now I realize as soon as I say the word "deliverance," the movie buffs among you are hearing banjo music but do try not to let that distract you too much.

"But" we say. Lead us not into temptation BUT deliver us from evil. I want to consider for a moment this short but significant word "but," so easy to overlook. It's a simple conjunction and yet Scripture is full of many very important uses of this simple conjunction that significantly shifts things, turns things upside down. This is why if anyone ever says to you: "I love you, but…" look out, you might need to make different plans for Valentine's Day. Or when people try to defend themselves against being called a racist by saying: "I'm not racist, but…" you can bet they're not going to be very convincing. In the Bible we often get the word "but" or "yet" at the moment when things look dark or discouraging, but *(see what I did there?)* then, we are reminded of God's love and God's salvation, and so it is in today's phrase in the Lord's Prayer.

"Lead us not into temptation," acknowledges that this world is full of tests and temptations – BUT – we shift things – "but deliver us from evil." So what is evil? I suspect each of us might come up with very different ideas of what is evil. It is worth noting that the Greek word used here covers a wide umbrella of things – from just the general idea of evil all the way to the idea of "The Evil One," a distinct being who directs and promotes the doing of evil. In fact some English translations of the Lord's Prayer use that language and translate this phrase as "deliver us from The Evil One," the personification of evil, the Devil.

I want to move on quickly because I do not think it matters whether you believe that evil comes from and is directed by some personified being who sits on your shoulder and encourages you to do evil things or that evil resides in each of our hearts and causes us to fall into doing evil. I don't think it really matters – the idea here is that we want to be delivered from evil, in whatever way, shape, or form it might manifest itself wherever it originates.

Most of the great Christian theologians would and did argue that evil is not something that exists in and of itself; evil is the opposite of, the lack of, the absence of, good. So what is good? Well - love, joy, peace, harmony, health, unity, laughter – the qualities that God and the Trinity exhibit. It is the absence of these qualities, the opposite of them, that defines evil. Suffering, pain, gossip, slander, malice, ridicule, disharmony, despair – these are symptoms of evil. Evil is anything that causes us to be drawn away from the Good, anything that gets between us and the Good; anything, then, that gets between us and God, is evil, or potentially evil.

So deliver us, God, we pray, from anything, that's going to get between our relationship with You, our pipeline to the Good. And that covers a wide area. When it comes to thinking about evil and good, you might think of it in terms of light and darkness. What is darkness? It is the absence of light. We wouldn't, for example, know what darkness was if the sun never rose, if we never saw its light. Darkness is the absence of light, we notice darkness when the light is not there, like when your power goes out. So it is with evil. It is the absence of goodness. And you can probably think of times in your life when you felt like you were in darkness, when you felt the absence of light and goodness, when it felt like goodness, and even God, was far away. So we pray, for such times: "deliver us from evil." Notice we don't say "destroy evil" or "take away all evil," we say, "deliver us from evil."

Remember Jesus taught us this prayer. Jesus Christ who some people thought would show up as a great warrior on a big white horse slaying all the Romans, slaying all our enemies, putting to death all those we think of as evil, and yet he didn't. Jesus came teaching love. He taught us how to overcome evil with good. So we aren't taught by Jesus to pray: "destroy evil" but "deliver us from evil." "Deliver us." When I hear the word "deliver," I think about mail or packages - things that get delivered. What does that mean? Well, it means something that starts in one place and ends up somewhere else. If the post office called you and said: "All your mail has been sitting in a storeroom here for six months," I suspect you wouldn't be thrilled at their great delivery service. To be accurately delivered something has got to get from one place to the other. So we pray to God: "deliver us from a place of evil, a place where we feel surrounded by evil, to a place of goodness, to your kingdom. Deliver us, move us, from this place to another place."

Does that happen here in this world or are we talking about the next life? Yes. Both. I mean, I don't know. But I do know this – in this prayer we are asking to be moved from wherever we feel surrounded and possibly overcome by evil to a place, a situation, a state of being, in which we will feel less so...whatever that might mean to the specific person praying it. The important thing, I think, is that we acknowledge the divine postal worker who will deliver us. We are like packages in this sense. If you have a package you want delivered to your Great Aunt who lives in Spokane, and you put it out on your porch, it is going to simply sit there on your porch. The package will not deliver itself. And so it is for us. We are like packages…who need someone to deliver us from a place of evil to a place of goodness. And so we turn to God.

We acknowledge that we live in a world full of all sorts of evil – suffering, pain, disease, violence – some of it comes from within ourselves, some of it comes from forces outside of us – but we know we live in such a place and we want to go, we long to go, somewhere else, to a place of goodness and peace. We can't do it ourselves, God, so be our refuge, be our fortress, be our deliverer—if not immediately, then someday. Let us know we are not alone, and that there is light and hope and salvation and deliverance, despite all the things in this world that tell us otherwise. That's why we turn to you, O God.

I want to end with some words from the great early Christian theologian and Bishop of the third century Cyprian, and quote what Cyprian said about this particular phrase in the Lord's Prayer: *"When we have once asked for God's protection against evil and have obtained it, then against everything which the devil and the world can do against us, we stand safe and secure. For what fear is there in this life to the [person] whose Guardian…is God?"*

These words we pray are words of profound trust and hope and confidence, not in ourselves or our goodness or our abilities or our accomplishments, but in our God, our Deliverer, who truly does deliver us from evil.

Amen.

Oh, Yes!

Revelation 22:20-21; 2 Corinthians 1:18-22

October 4, 2015

We come to the end of the Lord's Prayer, but I wanted to take one final Sunday to talk about this little word we use a lot: "Amen." We say it at the end of most of our prayers, perhaps without even really thinking about it.

Our English word derives ultimately from and is a transliteration of a Hebrew word: "*amen*". This Hebrew word denotes certainty, truthfulness, even faithfulness. There is a related verb in Hebrew, "*aman*," which means "to confirm" or "to uphold" something – "amen" is a word of affirmation. That's why we say "amen" at the end of our prayers. Jesus sometimes used this word (*not the English one, obviously*) at the beginning of what he would say, and in English we generally translate that as "truly" or in older translations "verily." "Truly I tell you…"

It is a word that means: "so be it." Or I think of what Mary says to the angel Gabriel when he comes and tell she that she's going to have a baby – God's baby – do you remember what Mary says in response, her declaration of trust in all that is about to happen? "Let it be with me according to your word." Now Mary doesn't use the word "amen" here, but I think her response is a pretty good summary of what the word really means: "let it be, God." "So be it." I also admire the way Eugene Peterson translates this word; in these two verses of Revelation 22 in **The Message**, he translates the first "amen" as "Yes!" and the second one as "Oh, Yes!" I like that – "Oh, yes!"

This little word is an affirmation, maybe THE great affirmation. When we end our prayers with "amen" we are saying that now we give all that we have prayed about to God, certain that God will respond to our requests...maybe not exactly the way we envision or expect, or as quickly as we'd like, but we affirm our certainty that God will respond and take care of things. So be it! Let it be! Oh, yes!

Give us and everyone this day what we need, our daily bread. Oh yes!

Let us stay out of time of testing and temptation and be delivered from evil in all its forms. Oh yes!

And so as we end this beautiful prayer, we conclude all that we say in the Lord's Prayer and in all our prayers with this simple but profound "amen," "so be it," "oh yes!"

This is why Eugene Peterson's translation has been stirring around inside me, and why it ties in so well with our passage from 2 Corinthians, where Paul declares, "our message to you was not "yes" and "no," it was "YES,"" because that's God's message, that's the message of Jesus Christ. In Christ it is not "yes" and "no," it's "YES." The message of Christ is "YES." God is a God of "YES." "Oh, Yes!"

One of the real problems with the Church since Day One has been turning a God of YES into a God of NO. How many of you were brought up with or still think of God as a God of NO? *"NO, DON'T DO THAT."*

"NO, DON'T SAY THAT."

"NO, DON'T QUESTION THAT"

"NO, DON'T EVEN THINK ABOUT THAT."

"NO"

"NO"

"NO"

But God is a God of "YES!" Within reason, of course. God doesn't want us to be stupid, but God is a God of YES. "LIVE! ENJOY! RELISH! SAVOR! TRY! YES, step outside your comfort zone. YES, even though I know you've never done it that way before. Don't worry, I AM here with you, so, YES, go for it!"

Not only have we turned God into a God of NO, but many of us as people are "NO" people.

"NO. It won't work. We've never done it that way before..."

Saying this little word "amen" reminds us of God's YES. Reminds us that God is a God of the attempt, of the possible and even the impossible - of faith, of change, of opportunity, of rebirth and renewal, of excitement and inspiration and the chance to start over and try again, of second chances and 312th chances. Reminds us that God is a God of miracles and surprises and new songs and unexpected victories. "Oh, Yes!"

And when you find yourself wrestling with some of those deep existential questions we often ask ourselves I think it is helpful to remember God's "YES."

Is there a God? YES!

Is there really hope? YES!

Will there ever really be peace...in our world, in our communities, in our families, in our own hearts? YES!

Will all be well, and all manner of things be well? YES.

Does God love you? YES!

This week I invite you to live with this little word "amen," God's "YES." And to not just live with it but find some times to use it. You know there are churches and congregations where people not only use it, they use it with enthusiasm and gusto: "Amen!!!!" It is good for us Presbyterians to do that once in a while, to yell out a good, old-fashioned, Pentecostal

"Amen!" Gets air into our lungs, and maybe even a bit more of the Spirit than usual. So surprise someone this week – if they say something you really agree with, instead of just saying: "Fine, that really sounds perfectly acceptable," say: "AMEN! Oh Yes!" And notice the reaction you'll get…if nothing else it should be fun to try it.

I invite you - encourage you - to live with God's "YES" this week.

I was thinking a lot about this, and I hate to admit it, but I realized what a negative person, a person of "NO" I tend to be. It's far too easy to fall into that trap of negativity in our world today, to just discount anything that seems too good to be true or too big a change to be possible.

But this week, carry this little word "amen" with you. It's a word that is easy to carry around with you- short, easy to remember, but difficult to misplace, unlike your cell phone. Carry it with you this week. In your prayers and in your heart especially. Maybe you want to wait until everyone else has left the house, but this week pray and then end with "AMEN!" As loud as you can yell it. Use your outside voice, just to be sure God hears you, and maybe the neighbor's too. "OH YES!" "I know you are with me, God, I know you can do what I am asking, and I leave it in your hands, and I'll try to do my part in the meantime." "Oh, Yes!" "Amen."

Let's work on being God's "Yes" people in a world so full of "NO".

Can I get an amen?

CPSIA information can be obtained
at www.ICGtesting.com
Printed in the USA
LVHW030327240520
656396LV00007B/533